The Legends & Lands of
Ireland

Richard Marsh

PHOTOGRAPHY BY ELAN PENN
FOREWORD BY FRANK McCOURT

Sterling Publishing Co., Inc. New York
A Sterling/Penn Book

Jeanette Green, Series Editor
Design and Cartography by Michel Opatowski
Copyedited by Felicia Miller

Library of Congress Cataloging-in-Publication Data

Marsh, Richard, 1939–
  Legends & lands of Ireland / Richard Marsh; photography by Elan Penn.
     p. cm.
  Includes bibliographical references and index.
  ISBN 1-4027-0784-3
  1. Folklore—Ireland. 2. Legends—Ireland. 3. Tales—Ireland.
  4. Ireland—Pictorial works. I. Title: Legends and lands of Ireland. II. Penn, Elan. III. Title.
GR147.M37 2003
398'.09417—dc21   2003006723

1 3 5 7 9 10 8 6 4 2

Published by Sterling Publishing Co., Inc.
387 Park Avenue South, New York, NY 10016

Penn Publishing, Ltd.
20 Hatichon St., P.O. Box 2190, Savyon, Israel 56530

ISBN 1-4027-0784-3

Cover photo: Blarney Castle, County Cork.
Title page photo: Hill of Skreen, County Meath. Ruins of Church of Skreen.

This book is dedicated to the poets, storytellers, monastic scribes, and folktale collectors of centuries past, who transmitted and preserved these stories so that we may enjoy them today, and especially to modern storytellers, who keep the stories alive by telling them.

Contents

Ireland

Foreword
by Frank McCourt

Jeremiah Curtin, an Irish-American anthropologist, asked an old Irishwoman if she believed in fairies and leprechauns and such creatures. She said, "I do not, but they're there."

My own mother, the late Angela Sheehan McCourt, would certainly have understood. She was a Catholic and a pagan. When her mother died, she claimed she'd heard the banshee wailing the night before. I was a skeptical fifteen-year-old and said that was nonsense. My mother's response was a "clitther" (a slap) on the jaw that sent me reeling. I should have known better.

Of course, she'd deny the pagan part, though she would have been hard put to explain her behavior on Bonfire Night—May Eve, the last night in April. In my childhood people in the lanes and backstreets of Limerick built bonfires. They gathered round the fires, drank porter or sherry—whatever they could afford—sang and told stories till the early hours. My uncle told me that a long time ago barren women would jump over the dying fire, and sure enough, nine month later, babies were born through the kindness of the fire. I didn't say nonsense to my uncle because he told that story with a twinkle that said take it or leave it.

When the fire burned low, my mother and the other women scooped up embers on shovels or into metal buckets. We followed my mother down the lane and around the house saying Hail Marys and sprinkling holy water.

If you had asked the women why they did that they would have said, "Well, that's what you do and that's all there is to it." It's the answer you would have received from Shirley Jackson's characters in her classic short story "The Lottery," where families in a New England town stoned one of their number every year.

In my childhood we knew little of Hans Christian Andersen, Charles Perrault, and the Brothers Grimm till Disney sent us the word. Instead we had thousands of years of lore, legend, song, story. Our heads were filled with the contents of the book you hold in your hand. We grew up with Cúchulainn and Fionn, our epic heroes, but not until we grew older (and savvier?) did we realize how cleverly Mother Church had co-opted our heroes. We were told Cúchulainn died on Good Friday in a rage over a dream he had—the crucifixion of Jesus. We were told that Oisín, of the Fianna, died when he fell off a horse while helping a monk lift a stone.

Indeed, the priests worked mightily to root out traces of old ways, old beliefs. They condemned bonfires, but not too vehemently. (They condemned drink, too, but again, not too vehemently.) They condemned wakes, especially in the country where poteen was taken and the young danced to the ditches and showed nature how to do it. They condemned dancing and managed to bring it from crossroads to dance halls where they could control it and tell the young, "Take your hands off that girl."

The Legends & Lands of Ireland is a book for slow times, a journey through the collective unconscious of the Irish race. You cannot speed through Richard Marsh's rich, nourishing prose, witty, learned, beautiful. If you do, you'll miss nuggets along the way. Linger a moment over the story of Cromwell's body (p. 143). Mr. Marsh carries his learning lightly, so lightly you might not notice how profound his scholarship is. He moves you from pre-Christian times into the wonderful stories of Saints Patrick, Kevin, and Brigit. Such contradictions, such ironies, such humor.

After centuries "under the Saxon heel," some Irish are becoming reflective, taking to the couch and musing on the past, not as victims lamenting and threatening to "rise up," but as an educated people with the leisure and intelligence to wonder how they arrived at this place, this state of mind.

Prosperity can be a threat to memory, but that threat is dismissed by books like this, especially when a photographer like Elan Penn supplies images of places throbbing with tradition and lore. Each picture here is worth a book in itself and every sentence of Richard Marsh is worth a picture.

—Frank McCourt

Irish-American author Frank McCourt won the Pulitzer Prize and the National Book Critics Circle Award for *Angela's Ashes: A Memoir* (1996), a memoir of his childhood in Limerick, Ireland. This bestseller was by followed by his sequel, *'Tis: A Memoir* (1997). Mr. McCourt's *The Irish…and How They Got That Way*, an Off-Broadway revue, premiered at the Irish Repertory Theatre in Manhattan in 2001 and has toured the United States and Australia.

Introduction

The lore and learning of Ireland, which included law, genealogy, myth, and a good deal of legend thoroughly mixed with factual history, were in the keeping of the *filid*, usually translated as "poets." These men combined the duties of druid, poet, lawyer, judge, genealogist, historian, and royal advisor in one office with specialized branches. Their training ranged broadly over the arts and sciences, including an intensive study of verse forms and the intricate Secret Language of the Poets. Only in their final years did they learn magic spells.

It took 12 years of study to become an *ollamh*, the top level of seven. The word literally means "prepared" and is the Modern Irish term for "university professor." An *ollamh* had to know perfectly 250 major stories and 100 minor ones. Although a 12th century manuscript lists the titles of 500 tales and poems, only about 200 are known today.

The Written Sources of the Stories: The Annals and Books

Until the Latin alphabet arrived with Christianity, there was no form of writing in Ireland, and the poets' lore was passed on orally. The story of Irish civilization, a mixture of history, myth, and legend, was first committed to writing in the sixth century by monks, who at least half-believed that what they recorded had really happened. It is often said of Irish storytellers past and present that they never let facts get in the way of a good story.

Five major annals survive, the largest of which, the 17th century *Annals of the Four Masters*, runs to some 430,000 words. The annals are a marvelous compendium of fact and fancy. They often begin with Adam and move on to the landing of the first people in Ireland and continue into the late Middle Ages. The lives, accomplishments, and deaths of legendary personages such as Fionn mac Cumhaill (d. A.D. 284), the Tuatha Dé Danaan

Howth Castle, Dublin.

(godlike superheroes), pre-Christian heroes, Christian saints, mythical and historical kings, and local abbots and bishops, as well as various raids, invasions, plagues, and astronomical and world events, are all recorded with democratic earnestness.

While the annals record historical facts and legendary events in chronological diary form, the other major written sources, usually called "Books," are miscellaneous anthologies or miniature libraries containing stories of history, legend, myth, and historical fiction, often illustrated with scraps of poems much older than the prose. The 12th century "Book of the Dun Cow" and "Book of Leinster" are the oldest important story manuscripts. Eight others dating from the 14th to the 17th century are generally more complete and better preserved.

The Story Cycles

The ancient storytellers organized stories by type: battles, voyages, violent deaths, overseas or Otherworld adventures, wooings, elopements, etc. Modern academics find it convenient to group the major stories in more or less chronological cycles: the Mythological Cycle, 3000 B.C. to A.D. 1; the Ulster Cycle, around the time of Christ; the Fionn Cycle, second to third centuries A.D.; and the Cycles of the Kings, third century B.C. to the 11th century A.D. Historical and legendary characters often appear in more than one cycle.

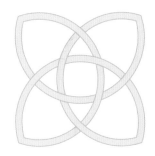

The Mythological Cycle

All cultures have a creation myth, an account of how the universe, humans, and animals came to be. The Irish creation myth was replaced by the Judeo-Christian account when medieval monks sanitized mythological history. But some scraps of the vanished myth can be detected in stories of the magical Tuatha Dé Danaan, the Tribes of the Goddess Dana.

For example, their chief or king, the *Dagda Mór*, "The Great Good-at-Everything God," possesses attributes of a sun or fire god. He mates with *Boann*, "White Cow," a moon or water goddess figure for whom the River Boyne is named. They live at the Otherworld palace known to us mortals as the Neolithic passage tomb at Newgrange on the bank of the Boyne. Opposites merge—fire and water, male and female—and produce a son, *Aengus Óg*, the god of love and youth. (See "The Dagda and Boann.") The Dagda also mates once a year with the Mórrígan, "Great Queen," an aspect of the Triple Goddess—virgin, mother, wise old woman. The Mórrígan is also a member with Badhbh and Macha of the battle goddess trinity called the Mórrígna. (See "The Second Battle of Moytura.").

As long as the Tuatha Dé Danaan were not called gods or seen to usurp the properties of the Christian God, they were deemed safe enough as magical superheroes living in the Otherworld, and stories about them remained in the collections.

The framework for the mythological history of Ireland is the *Lebor Gabála Erenn*. This book is usually called the "Book of Invasions of Ireland" in English, but *gabála* in this context is more accurately translated as "colonizations." The book is a fanciful account of the six groups of people who settled in Ireland before the coming of Christianity.

Although archaeology records Mesolithic inhabitants around 5000 B.C., according to mythological history the first people in Ireland were a party led by Cesair, granddaughter of Noah, who arrived with fifty women and three men 2,342 years after the creation of the world (*i.e.*, 2958 B.C.), 40 days before the Deluge. They all perished in the Deluge, and Ireland was empty for 278 years until the coming of Partholon and his people from Greece. After defeating the Fomorians, sea pirates who used Ireland as a base, the Partholonians were exterminated 300 years later by a plague. Ireland lay empty again for thirty years until the coming of Nemed and his followers from Scythia. The Nemedians occupied Ireland for 216 years until a great battle with the Fomorians killed nearly everyone on both sides, and the few remaining Nemedians left. Ireland was once more empty for 200 years until the Fir Bolg, descendants of the surviving Nemedians, occupied the country in 1934 B.C.

The Tuatha Dé Danaan overcame the Fir Bolg 37 years later and banished them to the West of Ireland and the islands, but the Fir Bolg remained an identifiable group. Ferdia, Cúchulainn's best friend, whom he fought and killed in the epic *Táin Bó Cuailnge*, "Cattle Raid of Cooley," was a Fir Bolg, and the Clan Morna, traditional rivals of Fionn mac Cumhaill's Clan Baiscne, were Fir Bolgs. Even today, some people in the West of Ireland proudly claim Fir Bolg ancestry, though elsewhere the term "Fir Bolg mentality" is used as "hillbilly mentality" is in the United States. The Tuatha Dé Danaan fought a great battle, the Second Battle of Moytura, with the Fomorians and defeated them. The Dagda then ruled as king for 80 years, until he died of a wound he had received at Moytura.

Although the Tuatha Dé Danaan had studied the magic arts "in the northern islands of Europe," they were a Bronze Age people, and their weapons were no match for those of the Iron Age Milesians, who arrived in 1699 B.C. from Spain. Having defeated the Tuatha Dé Danaan, the Milesians generously divided Ireland equally between the two peoples. They kept the upper half for themselves and gave the underground half to the Danaans. Manannán mac Lir taught the Danaans how to come and go into the hills and mounds, which are called *sidhe* or "fairy mounds" and are entrances to the Otherworld. For this reason the Danaans later became known as the people of the *sidhe*. As Christianity grew, the Sidhe people diminished in importance and size until they became the modern fairies, who live in "a land where even the old are fair, /And even the wise are merry of tongue."—from W. B. Yeats, *The Land of Heart's Desire* (1894)

Many folklorists say that "Spain" is used in Irish legends and folktales as a generic term for any faraway place or the Otherworld, but the "Spain" that the Milesians came from really means Spain. It is a historical fact that the Celts dominated the Iberian Peninsula from about 1000 to 500 B.C. The mythological history of Galicia, the northwest region of Spain, agrees with the mythological history of Ireland that the first Celts came to Ireland from Galicia, though the date of 1699 B.C. is not practical. Historians say groups of Celts arrived in Ireland between 1000 and 300 B.C., and the Celts as a significant cultural entity abandoned Spain about 500 B.C. Because of this connection, Irish lords exiled after a failed 16th century rebellion went to Spain and claimed Spanish citizenship.

Corcomroe Abbey, Ballyvaughan, County Clare. Effigy of King Conor O'Brien (d. 1267), a benefactor of the abbey. The niche where the effigy is placed is said to be Conor's burial place.

The Ulster Cycle

The Ulster Cycle, set about the time of Christ, consists of a collection of stories about the heroic deeds and deaths of a dozen or so kings and warriors. It is violent, bloody, and spiced with grisly black humor. The centerpiece of this cycle is the *Táin Bó Cuailnge*, "The Cattle Raid of Cooley," "the queen of Irish epic tales, and the wildest and most fascinating saga-tale, not only of the entire Celtic world, but even of all western Europe."[1] Many stories of *tánta*—cattle raids—survive, but the *Táin Bó Cuailnge* stands so high above the others that it is usually simply called the *Táin*.

It is known as the national epic of Ireland, but in fact it is the story of the defense of Ulster—more or less modern Northern Ireland—against an invasion by the rest of Ireland, so it is specifically the epic of Ulster. The story of how the *Táin* came to be written down both demonstrates the importance of the epic and "proves" its veracity.

The chief poet of Ireland, Senchán Tórpeist, decided to test the famed generosity of Guaire Aidhne, king of Connacht 655–666 (see other Guaire stories), and he set off on the Great Visitation to Guaire with 150 poets, 150 minor poets, 150 hounds, 150 servants, 150 women, and 27 people of every craft. They stayed a year and made outrageous demands, but law and custom prohibited Guaire from telling them to leave.

Guaire's brother, Marbán, a holy man whose pet white pig had been sacrificed to a whim of Senchán's wife, suggested a plan to get rid of them. Marbán knew that the poets of Ireland had forgotten the *Táin*, and when Guaire asked them to recite it and they couldn't, he was legally entitled to dismiss them and ban them from practicing their profession until they had learned it. They searched all over Ireland and Europe as far as Rome unsuccessfully, and they were on their way back to Guaire to admit their failure and plead with him to lift his ban.

When they stopped to rest, one of the poets leaned against an *ogham* stone (a stone inscribed in *ogham*, the earliest form of writing in Ireland). Out of curiosity, he read the inscription: "Here lies Fergus mac Roich." Fergus was a major character in the story of the *Táin* from beginning to end. The poets performed a ceremony and called Fergus's spirit from the Otherworld. He recited the *Táin*, and this time a scribe wrote it down.

Much of the *Táin* consists of pre-tellings, or in current film and fiction terminology, back-stories. The main plot is simple. Queen Maeve wanted to equal in wealth her husband, Aillil, who owned the White-Horned Bull. To do so, she needed the Brown Bull of Cooley (the Carlingford Peninsula,

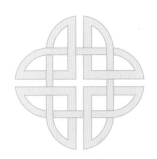

Sheep grazing on Corraun Peninsula, Achill Sound, County Mayo.

now part of County Louth in the Republic, but then part of Ulster). A pre-telling explains how two rival druids had shape-changed into these two greatest bulls in Ireland. Maeve asked the king of Cooley for the Brown Bull, but he refused, and so she assembled her warriors and those of her allies, invaded Ulster, and took the Brown Bull. When she brought it back to Connacht, the two bulls fought and killed each other.

As soon as Maeve and her army set off for Ulster, the men of Ulster fell victim to the Curse of Macha, and 17-year-old Cúchulainn, immune to the curse because of his youth and his divine parentage, was left to defend Ulster single-handed. Many of the back-stories of the *Táin*, as well as other non-*Táin* tales of the Ulster Cycle, concern Cúchulainn, who to this day personifies the quintessential Irish hero. Besides the obvious literary and cultural reasons for this, there are two that are political.

Patrick Pearse was the leader of the 1916 Easter Rising, which led to the War of Independence. He was a devout Catholic, patriot, and poet, whose heroes were Jesus Christ and Cúchulainn because they had given their lives for their people. The British executed ("canonized," as George Bernard Shaw put it) Pearse and 15 other rebels, and their martyrdom provided the main impetus that led to Irish independence. In his poem "Renunciation," Pearse showed clearly his intention to follow his heroes' path of blood sacrifice:

> "I have turned my face
> To this road before me,
> To the deed that I see
> And the death I shall die."

Mortally wounded, Cúchulainn tied himself to a pillar so he would die standing and facing his enemies. This image is at the center of Desmond Kinney's 1974 glass and ceramic mosaic mural, *The Táin*, on the side of the Northern Ireland Tourist Board's office on Nassau Street in Dublin. The panorama faces the Setanta Centre office building—Cúchulainn's original name was Sétanta—and illustrates major events in the hero's career.

Probably a deliberate parallel with the figure of Christ on the cross, a central icon in Catholicism, the Death of Cúchulainn is a central icon of Irish nationalism. It is for this reason that the bronze sculpture of that name, by Pearse's friend Oliver Sheppard, was installed on Easter Monday 1935 in the General Post Office (GPO) on Dublin's O'Connell Street, where the Rising began. Yeats noted this connection in one of his last poems, "The Statues":

Cliffs of Moher, County Clare

"When Pearse summoned Cuchulain to his side,
What stalked through the Post Office?"

Also, in Yeats's 1939 verse play *The Death of Cuchulain*:

"What stood in the Post Office
With Pearse and Connolly?...
A statue's there to mark the place,
By Oliver Sheppard done."

Cúchulainn is an iconic figure for Protestants in Northern Ireland for a parallel but opposite reason. Protestants are a two-thirds majority there—one million of the 1.5 million in the province. They would be a 20 percent minority—one million of the five million in the entire island—in a united Ireland. To Protestant Unionists or Loyalists, who wish to remain part of the United Kingdom, a united Ireland would be tantamount to the invasion and conquest of Ulster by the rest of Ireland. Cúchulainn single-handedly defended Ulster against an invasion 2,000 years ago, and so it is ironic but fitting to find large murals called "gable art" in Loyalist neighborhoods in the North depicting the same Death of Cúchulainn scene found in the GPO in Dublin.

The Fionn Cycle

Fionn mac Cumhaill is the hero of the common people, a warrior who falls in love, weeps for a lost lover and a dead grandson, and has to be extracted from peril. In a 19th century literary burlesque (see "Fionn and the Scottish Giant"), he is a cowardly buffoon whose wife, Clever Oonagh, rescues him from an unwise challenge to a Scottish giant.

Perhaps the greatest tribute to Fionn's lasting popularity is a defense by one of the early translators of the manuscripts, Eugene O'Curry, in the 19th century:

"It is quite a mistake to suppose him to have been a merely mythical character. Much that has been narrated of his exploits is, no doubt, apocryphal enough; but Finn himself is an undoubtedly historical personage; and that he existed about the time at which his appearance is recorded in the annals, is as certain as that Julius Caesar lived and ruled at the time stated on the authority of the Roman historians."[2]

The Cycles of the Kings (also called the Historical Cycle)

These are groups of stories based on several kings. The seventy or so stories in these cycles range from the third century B.C. to the 11th century A.D. Some of the kings were historical personages, and many of the stories are based on fact. Some accounts are little more than genealogical records, but several bear the mark of the court poet or storyteller's conscious craftsmanship. Migrant international legends are often artistically attached to the ancestors of the teller's patron to display his heroic qualities, and the royal lineage can be unashamedly traced back through prominent characters of history, legend, and myth to Adam.

These cycles are represented in this book by stories about the last pagan high king, Diarmait mac Cerbaill, and the first Christian high king, Cormac mac Art. Another story about Diarmait, "The Cursing of Tara," is included in Chapter 4, "Legends of Saints."

The Legends in Modern Ireland

The Irish are often accused of living in the past, and considering the richness of the distant past of heroic story and the misery of the intermediate past under British rule, it is quite understandable that they have preferred to identify themselves with glory rather than subjugation. Even now, nearly a century after independence, myth and legend thrive in the national consciousness, especially through the arts, to the extent that it could be said that one of the most modern things about 21st century Ireland is the homage paid to its legendary history.

Here are a few of the more public examples. A monumental statue of Cúchulainn and Ferdia has recently been erected on the main street of Ardee, County Louth, near the ford where their single combat took place, and a bronze plaque has been fixed on the commemorative stone Maeve and Aillil placed at the ford 2,000 years ago. A ballet of the *Táin*, sculptures of the bulls that are central to the epic, the *Death of Cúchulainn* statue in Dublin's main post office and gable art in the North, the mosaic mural *The Táin* in Dublin, and plays and poems by Yeats and other writers continue to recycle the story. *An Poc Fada* ("The Long Hurley-Stroke") is an annual competition in Cúchulainn's territory in County Louth, in which contestants hit a *sliotar* ("hurling ball") along part of the *Táin* route with as few strokes as possible, as the young Cúchulainn did on his way to Emain Macha. An Poc Fada is also the name of a Dublin pub.

In 2002, *Diarmuid and Gráinne*, a gun-toting Bonnie and Clyde comedy version of the Fionn Cycle saga billed as "an ancient tale of sex, drugs and rock 'n' roll," played in a Dublin theater after a successful tour of the country, and the legendary-historical 16th century pirate queen of Connacht, Granuaile, was the subject of a stage production. James Joyce's *Finnegan's Wake*, inspired by Fionn mac Cumhaill, is one of the great literary works of the 20th century. Other examples are the majestic *Children of Lir* statue in the Garden of Remembrance in Dublin, 1970s rock operas *The Book of Invasions* and *The Táin* by Horslips, and the profusion of fantasy novels based on Irish myth and legend themes and characters.

The influence of Irish stories extends outside the country. A notable example is the central motif in the Diarmuid and Gráinne saga and the story of Deirdre, which is the source of the Tristan and Isolde story of the Arthurian Cycle and Wagner's opera. Another example is found in Mark Helprin's New York novel *Winter's Tale* (1983), where the Irish-born hero draws his sword, neatly quarters an airborne apple with it, and cleans the sword and returns it to his belt without being seen to move. This act is remarkably similar to Cúchulainn's "apple feat," one of his warrior stunts meant to impress an enemy.

Unlike sacred myth in some cultures, which is as unchangeable as the Gospel of Jesus, Irish legends can be found in a number of forms. The versions of the stories that I tell and that are in this book are all traditional, with the exception of the literary "Fionn and the Scottish Giant." They are the versions that make most sense to me as a storyteller, that allow me and my audiences to most easily suspend disbelief.

Are the Stories True?

The prominent 20th century academic Myles Dillon acknowledged that "there is a great deal of history" in the Cycles of the Kings, and that through these legendary histories "a fairly reliable historical tradition can be established from as early a time as the second century of the Christian Era."[3] Many folklorists would not concur with Dillon that certain prominent legendary personages may well have been real people, but modern scholars agree that cultural and historical facts can be gleaned from stories in all the Cycles. Archaeological discoveries frequently corroborate these facts, and this is helped by the interest taken in myth and legend by the younger archaeologists, like their amateur antiquarian predecessors of the 19th century.

But more important than historicity is the reason these tales have survived in the consciousness and subconscious of modern Ireland, as have traditional stories in other societies. Scholarly books have been written and academic careers devoted to the subject, but the clearest explanation comes in the words of a child. A storyteller was telling stories to a group of children. At the end of one story, a young listener put the frequently asked question: "Is that story true?" Before the storyteller could answer, a five-year-old said, "It might not be true on the outside, but it's true on the inside."

Great Stone Circle, Lough Gur, County Limerick. This 4,000-year-old Bronze Age stone circle is the largest in Ireland at 150 feet (45 m) in diameter.

Chapter 1

Myths

The Naming of Baltinglass

The town of Baltinglass in Southwest County Wicklow was originally called Belach Dubhtaire ("Jungle Pass") for the road through the vast forests that existed in that region until the 12th century. This is the story of how it got its present name.

Drebrenn, a sister of Queen Maeve of Connacht, had three foster sisters who were married to three brothers. The mother of the girls did not approve of the match, and one day she transformed all six into pigs: the Demon Swine of Drebrenn.

The Swine lived for a time in the Cave of Cruachan near Maeve's royal seat in County Roscommon, but when they broke out they devastated Ireland.

One of the pigs was sighted near Tara, and Glas, Master of the Hounds for High King Etirscel the Great, leapt onto his horse and chased it southward, accompanied by his hound. The pig disappeared into a cave on Baltinglass Hill, and Glas and his horse and hound followed it, never to be seen again. That is how the hill and the town of Baltinglass got their present name: *Belach Con Glais,* the "Road of the Hound of Glas."

Baltinglass Hill, County Wicklow. Baltinglass was originally called Belach Dubhtaire, "Jungle Pass," for the dense forests that existed here until the 12th century. Its present name (Belach Con Glais, "Road of the Hound of Glas") derives from Glas's chase of one of the Demon Swine of Drebrenn into a cave on Baltinglass Hill. The ruins of a 12th century Cistercian monastery and a modern church can be seen in the foreground next to the River Slaney.

The Fate of the Children of Lir
One of the Three Sorrowful Tales of Ireland

Bobh Derg, son of the Dagda, was elected chief of the Tuatha Dé Danaan. Lir of Sidhe Fionnachaidh (near Newtownhamilton in County Armagh) had been a contender for the position, and to console him Bobh Derg offered his foster daughter Aobh for a wife. Aobh bore the twins Fionnuala, a girl, and Aed, a boy, and later died giving birth to the twin boys Fiachra and Conn. Bobh Derg offered Lir his other foster daughter, Aoife, Aobh's sister, for a wife.

Everyone loved the four Children for their engaging personalities and their sweet singing voices. Aoife also loved them and was a good stepmother for a time, but eventually, having no children of her own, she became envious of their popularity and decided to get rid of them. She didn't have the heart to kill them, but she took them on what she said was a visit to their Uncle Bobh Derg. She stopped at Lough Derravaragh in County Westmeath and changed them into swans.

Fionnuala, the eldest, protested at the injustice of this, and Aoife relented so far as to stipulate that they would remain in the form of swans for 300 years on Lough Derravaragh, 300 years on the Sea of Moyle between Ireland and Scotland, and 300 years on the Western Sea off the Mayo coast. They retained their human intelligence and voices.

When Lir discovered what had happened, he complained to Bobh Derg, who ordered Aoife to come before him.

"What is the punishment you dread most?" he asked her.

"To be changed into a demon of the air," she said.

"Then that is the punishment you shall have." And so it happened.

Lir and Bobh Derg and all the people of Ireland used to gather on the shores of Lough Derravaragh to listen to the sweet singing of the Children, but after 300 years the Children were forced by Aoife's spell to move to the stormy Sea of Moyle, and after another 300 years to the wind-swept Western Sea. Inishglora, off the Belmullet Peninsula, was their home until one day they heard a church bell. Christianity had arrived in Ireland.

They followed the sound of the bell and met with a disciple of Saint Patrick, to whom they told their story. He baptized them, and this broke Aoife's spell. As they changed back into human form, they immediately fell down and died of old age. This is the image depicted in Oisín Kelly's 1971 sculpture in the Garden of Remembrance in Parnell Square in Dublin.

Children of Lir by Oisín Kelly, Garden of Remembrance, Dublin. Fionnuala and her brothers return to human form as elderly people after 900 years as swans. The 25-foot (8-m) sculpture echoes the line from Yeats's poem, "Easter 1916": "All changed, changed utterly."

The Dagda and Boann

Irish passage tombs date from c. 4400 to 2500 B.C. According to mythological history, the magical Tuatha Dé Danaan built the passage tombs about 1800 B.C. Later the Tuatha Dé Danaan became known as the *Daoine Sidhe,* "People of the Mounds." Each sidhe (mound or passage tomb) is an

entrance to the Otherworld. Newgrange, a large passage tomb in County Meath on the bank of the River Boyne, is dated to 3200 B.C. The sun shines through a special window over the entrance to light up the chamber on five mornings at the Winter Solstice in December. Three of the Tuatha Dé Danaan, the water-goddess figure Boann, the sun-god figure Dagda, and their son, Aengus Óg, are associated with Newgrange.

Newgrange Passage Tomb, County Meath. Built about 3200 B.C., Newgrange is one of the largest and best-known passage graves in Europe.

Entrance Stone, Newgrange Passage Tomb, County Meath. This magnificent stone, measuring 10.5x4.25 feet (3.2x1.3 m), is generally considered the finest example of Neolithic (New Stone Age) art in Europe.

Boann was prohibited from going to the Well of Segais, a well of wisdom situated in the Curlew Hills on the Sligo-Roscommon border. This prohibition made her angry, so she went to the Well and walked around it three times *tuathal*, that is, counter-clockwise, as a form of protest. A left-turn circuit shows disrespect or challenge and is used in cursing rituals. The water took this as an insult and rose up against her, chasing her across the country to the Irish Sea. The route Boann took in her flight is now the course of the River Boyne, which is named after her.

When the Tuatha Dé Danaan had finished constructing the sidhe mounds, the Dagda looked around for one for himself to live in, and he chose Newgrange. The problem was that Boann and her husband, Elcmar, were already living there. The Dagda hit on a plan to get rid of the husband. He sent Elcmar on an errand that should have taken one day, but he stopped the sun for nine months. When Elcmar returned, thinking it was the evening of the day he had left, Boann was cradling a baby boy in her arms. "Isn't it wonderful," she said, "the baby who was conceived in the morning and born the evening of the same day."

This was Aengus Óg, "Young Aengus," the son of the Dagda. He is the god of youth and love, and the birds are his kisses. When Aengus was a young man, he asked the Dagda to give him Newgrange for a day and a night. The Dagda reckoned his son wanted to hold a party for his friends, so he made himself scarce. After a day and a night, he returned and said to Aengus, "I'll take Newgrange back now."

Aengus said, "But you gave it to me for all eternity."

"No, I didn't," said the Dagda. "I gave it to you for a day and a night."

"But all eternity is made of days and nights. Therefore, you gave it to me for all eternity."

The Dagda scratched his head and said, "That makes sense. All right, you can keep it." And he went off to find alternative accommodation. (Some say he settled at Grianán Aileach in Donegal.) That is why Newgrange is also called the Castle of Aengus.

The River Boyne at Slane Bridge, County Meath. The Boyne is named for the water goddess Boann, who was chased by water from the Well of Segais to the Irish Sea. The course taken by the water formed the river.

Grianán Aileach
The Sun Parlor of Aileach

Grianán Aileach, County Donegal. This hill fort near Derry City was the medieval stronghold of the O'Neills. According to legend, the Tuatha Dé Danaan met here to divide Ireland among themselves, and Aed, son of the Dagda, is buried here.

A medieval stronghold of the O'Neills, the majestic stone hill fort called Grianán Aileach occupies a site mentioned frequently in mythological history. This is where the Tuatha Dé Danaan met to divide Ireland among themselves, and where they killed Ith, uncle of Mil of the Celts of Spain, which instigated the Milesian invasion.

It is the burial site of the Danaan king, Nuada, and the resting place of the 16th century Ulster lord, Red Hugh O'Donnell. Legend has it that Hugh is not dead but will return some day to defend his people.

Some say that after the Dagda was ousted from Newgrange by his son Aengus, he came to live at the Grianán. The Dagda's son Aed Minbhrec is buried here. Aed was falsely accused by Corgenn of sleeping with his wife, and Corgenn murdered Aed in front of the Dagda at the Grianán. The Dagda would have been within his rights to kill Corgenn, but he chose the option of demanding another form of *eric*, or fine, as compensation. He required Corgenn to carry Aed's body around Ireland until he found a flat stone exactly the same length, width, and depth as the body to use as a memorial stone.

Corgenn tramped up and down the country until he arrived back at the Grianán, where he found the right-size stone next to the spot where he had killed Aed. Then his heart stopped and he died.

Ollamh Fodhla

The Loughcrew Passage Tomb Cemetery sprawls across three hills on the ridge called Sliabh na Caillí ("Hill of the Hag") between Crossakeel and Oldcastle in northwest County Meath. At the time the antiquary (amateur archaeologist) Eugene Conwell investigated it in 1863, it consisted of about a hundred passage tombs in various states of repair. About 30 remain. Basing his argument on a description in the 12th century *Lebor na hUidre*, Conway claimed that one of the tombs was the resting place of the poet-king Ollamh Fodhla, the 18th king of Ireland, who reigned in the 13th century B.C. This tomb, designated "Cairn T" by Conwell and modern archaeologists, is oriented to the rising sun at the autumnal and spring equinoxes, when a sunbeam enters through the passage to illuminate sun symbols carved on the back stone of the end recess in the chamber.

In a paper he read before the Royal Irish Academy in 1872 and published as a book the following year, Conwell explained:

> "What first led us to conceive the idea that this carn must be the tomb of Ollamh Fodhla was the fact of its having, as one of the thirty-seven large stones in the periphery of its base, a great stone chair facing the north, in our days popularly called 'The Hag's Chair'...we can well imagine how appropriately a great seat of justice was placed in the north side of the great lawmaker's tomb, from which, with all the solemnity attaching to the place, his laws

Loughcrew Passage Tomb Cemetery, Oldcastle, County Meath. Located between Crossakeel and Oldcastle, the Loughcrew Passage Tombs on the ridge called Sliabh na Caillí *("Hill of the Hag") date from the Neolithic period (c. 3000 B.C.). While local tradition designates the mound pictured here as the Witch's Cave, a 19th century antiquary believed it to be the tomb of the 13th century B.C. poet-king, Ollamh Fodhla.*

were administered, say at mid-day, with the recipients of the adjudications fully confronted with the great luminary, the object of their worship. For these reasons we propose, henceforth, to call this remarkable stone chair, emblazoned as it is, both on front and back, with characters at present perfectly unintelligible to us, 'Ollamh Fodhla's Chair.'"[4]

Ollamh Fodhla—obviously a title, not a personal name—is credited with establishing the first code of laws and a basic form of government. The *Annals of the Four Masters* have this to say about him:

1317 B.C.: The first year of the reign of Ollamh Fodhla, son of Fiacha Finscothach...

1277 B.C.: Ollamh Fodhla, after having been forty years in the sovereignty of Ireland, died at his own house at Teamhair [Tara].

He was the first king by whom the Feis Teamhrach [Feast of Tara] was established...It was he also that appointed a chieftain over every cantred, and a Brughaidh [guesthouse-keeper] over every townland, who were all to serve the King of Ireland. Eochaidh was the first name of Ollamh *Fodhla*; and he was called Ollamh Fodhla because he had been first a learned Ollamh [poet], and afterwards king of Fodhla, i.e., of Ireland.

The Loughcrew passage tomb complex has given rise to a local folk tale (see "The Hill of the Hag"), but little is known about Ollamh Fodhla, and there are no stories about him. However, the vacuum has been filled by two main branches of speculation, which amount to modern living legends.

The First Legend Since the circumstances of the death of the prophet Jeremiah are unknown, "he may as well have lived and died in Ireland as in any other country." He was the first bearer of the title *Ollamh Fodhla*. He brought the Lia Fáil (Jacob's Pillow), the Ark of the Covenant (containing the Torah), and King Zedekiah's daughter Teia (or Tamar) Tephi to Ireland in 583 B.C. Jeremiah taught the Dagda (d. 1749 B.C.), chief of the Irish demigods, the Tuatha Dé Danaan, how to administer the Torah. Teia (or Tamar) married the Dagda (whose personal name was Eochaid) and reigned as queen at Tara, where she is buried and which takes its name from her. The Ark of the Covenant is buried there. (In 1899 a group of British Israelites excavated extensively in search of it.) Deciphered carvings inside Ollamh Fodhla's Tomb say he died September 21, 581 B.C. On his death, the title of Ollamh Fodhla passed to the Dagda.

The Second Legend Ollamh Fodhla was King David (who died c. 962 B.C.), because not only did they reign for the same number of years, "*they reigned at the very same time in history!*" *Ollamh* is really the Hebrew word *olam*, which means "forever." *Tara* derives from *Torah*. The Tuatha Dé Danaan are the Tribe of Dan. A settlement near Tara called Dowd's Town is literally David's Town. And so on.

On a clear day, Ollamh Fodhla's Tomb can be discerned from the Hill of Tara—24 miles (40 km) to the southeast—as a pimple on Carnbane East, the middle hill of the three-hill ridge. A more dramatic view can be had from the crossroads at Crossakeel. Information about access to the interior of the mound is available from the Newgrange Visitors Centre.

The Second Battle of Moytura

Cesair, the Partholonians, the Nemedians, and the Fir Bolg had all come and occupied Ireland in their turn. About 1900 B.C., the Tuatha Dé Danaan defeated the Fir Bolg in the First Battle of Moytura, said to have taken place near Cong in County Galway. The Danaans' king, Nuada, lost a hand and therefore his right to the kingship in that conflict.

That is the background to the Second Battle of Moytura, the nearest approach in Irish tradition to a sacred mythology, in which godlike archetypal figures contend for supremacy. The battleground was the plain still designated Moytura or Moytirra on modern maps, east of Lough Arrow and southeast of Sligo Town. The entire area constitutes a sacred or ritual landscape and is the setting for a number of other mythological stories.

The Tuatha Dé Danaan had earlier made an alliance with the dreaded Fomorians, sea pirates from Scandinavia who had fought against the previous occupants of Ireland. Needing a king after Nuada's incapacitation, they elected Bres, half-Danaan and half-Fomorian. After seven years in office, Bres was forced from power because of his exorbitant taxes, enslavement of the Danaan leaders, and especially his stinginess, which even today is a character fault unacceptable to Irish people.

Meanwhile, the Danaan physician, Diancecht, fashioned a mechanical silver hand for Nuada, for which he is known as Nuada Silver-Hand. Diancecht's son Miach then healed the flesh-and-blood hand and reattached it to Nuada's arm in full working order. Diancecht killed Miach out of jealousy.

Bres sought help from the Fomorian champion Balor of the Evil Eye, who assembled a fleet that stretched like a bridge from Scandinavia to Ireland. Fearful of a prophecy that his grandson would kill him, Balor had imprisoned his only daughter, Eithne, in a tower on Tory Island. But Cian son of Diancecht found his way there. Their son was *Lugh Samildánach* ("of the Many Talents").

With Nuada healed and restored to the kingship, the Tuatha Dé Danaan were meeting in war council at Tara, when Lugh, who was not known to them, arrived at the door. The porter questioned him.

"What art do you practice? For no one without an art enters Tara."

Lugh enumerated his professions: builder, smith, champion, harper, warrior, poet, historian, sorcerer, physician, cupbearer, brazier. The porter said

View from the top of Heapstown Cairn, Castlebaldwin, County Sligo. During the Second Battle of Moytura, the Tuatha Dé Danaan put their mortally wounded warriors into the Well of Healing, and they could fight the following day. Their opponents, the Fomorians, heaped stones over the well so it could no longer be used, creating this huge cairn.

he was not needed and reeled off the names of Danaans who had those talents.

"But do you have any one person who possesses all those talents?" asked Lugh.

The porter went to confer with Nuada, who ordered that Lugh be admitted. The porter told Lugh he could enter, but Lugh leapt over the wall to prove that he could have entered without permission. This angered the Danaan champion, Ogma, who picked up a flagstone that required 80 yoke of oxen to move and hurled it through the wall. Lugh retrieved it and hurled it back so that it landed exactly where Ogma had torn it from, and he repaired the wall.

Nuada stepped down so Lugh could be temporary king and battle leader. The chief wizards and poets and craftsmen detailed how they would contribute their abilities in the coming battle. The wizard would cause the

Moytura, between Lough Arrow and Sligo Town, County Sligo. The major set piece of Irish mythology, the Second Battle of Moytura, took place in this area of County Sligo around 1800 B.C.

mountains to shake, so that the Fomorians would think the land was fighting on the side of the Tuatha Dé Danaan. The cupbearer would hide the water of the lakes and rivers from the enemy. The druid would rain fire on them, and so on.

The Dagda met with the Mórrígan, an aspect of the Mother Goddess and one of the triad of battle goddesses (with Macha and Badhbh) at the River Unshin, south of Collooney, and mated with her. (Some scholars consider this one of the few surviving scraps of an Irish creation myth overlooked by the Christian scribes who committed the stories to writing.) The Mórrígan promised to kill the Fomorian king, Indech.

The Dagda went to the Fomorian camp to ask for a truce to delay them while the Tuatha Dé Danaan prepared for battle. The Fomorians made a cauldron of porridge for him with 80 gallons of milk, added goats and sheep and swine, and poured it into a hole in the ground. Indech made him eat it. As he waddled away from the camp, he met Indech's daughter. A Rabelaisian scene ensues in which she mocks and beats the Dagda until he seduces her. She then agrees to kill a ninth part of the Fomorians.

During the battle, Diancecht and his two sons and daughter put mortally wounded Danaans into the Well of Healing and chanted spells over them, so that they were fit to fight again the following day. Ruadán, son of Bres and Brigit (daughter of the Dagda), wounded the smith Goibhniu, but he went into the Well and was healed. The Fomorians discovered the Well and heaped stones over it so it could no longer be used. This is Heapstown Cairn at the northwest end of Lough Arrow. Then the buck-toothed wife of Balor, Cethlenn, wounded the Dagda. He died 80 years later from the effects of the wound. Balor killed Nuada.

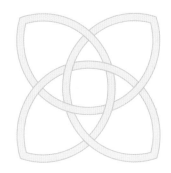

Balor's evil eye received its power from fumes of a druid's poisonous brew. It was only opened in battle, when four men were required to lift the lid. It would kill all who looked into it, so Lugh used a polished shield as a mirror and slung a stone through the eye, which then killed 27 Fomorians behind Balor. The battle was over. Nearly 100,000 Fomorian chiefs and nobles had been killed. Bres was spared when he promised to teach the Tuatha Dé Danaan the secrets of agriculture.

The Fomorians had carried off the Dagda's harp, Uaithne. He entered their camp, saw the harp hanging on the wall, and called it to him. It flew through the air, killing nine Fomorians. The Dagda then played the three kinds of music every accomplished musician can play: sorrow, joy, and sleep. When the Fomorians had fallen asleep, the Dagda made his escape safely.

Hill of Slane, County Meath.

Tales of Fionn mac Cumhaill and the Fianna

Aideen and Oscar

"Delightful it is to be at Benn Etar...
A hill on which Fionn and the Fianna used to meet,
A hill where horns and cups overflow...
The loveliest hill in Erin's isle."—*Anonymous*

The modern name of the Howth Peninsula north of Dublin derives from the Norse word for "headland." The Irish name is Ben Edar for the Tuatha Dé Danaan owner of the place and father of *Aideen Fholtfhind* ("Fair-Haired").

Fionn mac Cumhaill and the Fianna were in the Galtee Mountains in Munster one day when they were challenged by a Sidhe woman to a footrace to Ben Edar. She won, easily outstripping even Fionn's nephew, Caoilte the Swift, who had been known to run the length and breadth of Ireland so fast that he was not seen to leave and return. After the race, Fionn and the Fianna were invited to a feast in the sidhe of Edar, where Fionn was introduced to the beautiful and gentle Aideen, who was serving drinks. Her father told Fionn that Cairbre Liffechair, son of High King Cormac mac Art, had offered an extravagant bride-price to marry her—a cantred of land and his own weight in silver and gold. But this had been rejected.

"Why was that?" said Fionn.

"Because she feels neither inclination nor fondness for him, and besides, she has a lover of the Fianna whom she visits at night."

"Who might that be?" asked Fionn.

"Your own grandson, Oscar."

"What terms would you ask from us, for her to marry Oscar?"

Edar called Aideen and asked her, "My dear daughter, what terms do you ask of the chief of the Fianna for you to marry his grandson?"

"Only that he promise never to leave me, unless it be through my own fault."

"Goll mac Morna and I give you that promise on behalf of Oscar," said Fionn, "and our guarantee that he will keep it."

So Oscar and Aideen were married, and the feast turned into a wedding feast that lasted 20 days and nights.

Not long after that, the Battle of Ben Edar occurred, in which Oscar received such a serious wound that the Fianna were sure he would die. Aideen was sent for, and when she saw him lying gray and deathlike on his bed, she fell into despair and died of grief. She was buried at Ben Edar, where a large dolmen marks her grave.

However, Oscar, the strongest of the Fianna, recovered from his injuries to fight and die in the final battle of the Fianna, the Battle of Gabhra, in A.D. 284. (See "Fionn and the Battle of Gabhra.")

Diarmuid and Gráinne

*"Give to these children, new from the world, / Silence and love."—
from W. B. Yeats, "A Fairy Song—Sung by the people of Faery over Diarmuid and Grania, in their Bridal Sleep under a Cromlech,"
(1893)*

Diarmuid Ua Duibhne son of Donn, was the foster son of Aengus at Newgrange, and he lived there with Aengus. Donn's wife had a son, Gulbán, by another man, Roc, the steward at Newgrange, and this made Donn jealous. One day Aengus held a great feast. Diarmuid was there, and Donn and Roc and Gulbán. People were making a fuss over Gulbán, and this made Donn even more jealous. He threw meat among the dogs to start them fighting, and the men formed a circle to watch. When the boys, Diarmuid and Gulbán, crawled away from the dogfight through the men's legs, Gulbán went between the legs of Donn, and Donn squeezed his legs together and killed the boy. Roc brought him back to life in the form of a wild boar, and Gulbán went to live on the mountain north of Sligo Town called Ben Gulbáin (now Ben Bulben). And Roc put a curse on his son and Diarmuid: "You two will be the death of each other." Thereafter it was taboo for Diarmuid to go boar hunting.

Diarmuid became a member of the Fianna when he grew up, and he was so famed for his good looks he was called beautiful, even by men. Fionn mac Cumhaill, now an old man, was going to marry young Gráinne, daughter of High King Cormac mac Art. When all had assembled at Tara for the wedding, Gráinne saw Fionn for the first time and had doubts about the difference in their ages. Then she saw beautiful young Diarmuid and fell in love with him. She put a sleeping potion in everyone's wine but hers and Diarmuid's, and when everyone else was asleep, she took Diarmuid by the

Proleek Dolmen, in the grounds of Ballymascanlon Hotel, north of Dundalk, County Louth. This is an Early Bronze Age (2500 to 2000 B.C.) portal tomb, one of the most picturesque in Ireland. The capstone weighs 40 tons.

Poulnabrone Dolmen, The Burren, County Clare. This Bronze Age portal tomb or dolmen is the most frequently photographed megalithic tomb in Ireland. Diarmuid built a dolmen every night as a shelter for himself and Gráinne during the year and a day Fionn mac Cumhaill chased them.

two ears and put *geis* (an injunction of honor) on him to take her away with him.

Fionn, as Diarmuid's Fianna captain, was like a king to him. If Diarmuid took Fionn's intended wife, it would be like an act of treason. If he didn't do what Gráinne enjoined him to do, he would lose his honor. He chose honor over loyalty, and they set off. Fionn and the Fianna chased them around Ireland for a year and a day. Aengus came to them and advised them to sleep in a different place each night. Diarmuid built simple shelters of stone for Gráinne and himself every time they stopped to sleep, and that is why there were once 366 of what are now called dolmens or portal tombs (formerly "cromlechs") in Ireland. (Actually, only 175 remain.) Unable to catch them—Diarmuid had learned his warrior skills from Manannán mac Lir—the Fianna finally persuaded Fionn to forgive the lovers and allow them to return to Tara in safety.

One morning, Diarmuid heard the horns of the Fianna calling the men together for a boar hunt.

"I'm going boar hunting with the Fianna today," Diarmuid said to Gráinne.

"No, don't go," said Gráinne. "It's taboo for you."

But Diarmuid went anyway. The hunting that day happened to be at Ben Bulben, where Diarmuid's half-brother, the wild boar, lived. Some say Fionn planned it that way deliberately, but there is no evidence to prove that. However, it wasn't long before Diarmuid and Gulbán met. The boar charged Diarmuid, Diarmuid hurled his spear at the boar and dealt him a mortal wound, but the boar continued his charge and gave Diarmuid a mortal wound.

As Diarmuid lay dying, Fionn and the Fianna gathered around him. Fionn, as a sort of king and with demigod blood in his veins—he was the great-grandson of both Nuada of the Tuatha Dé Danaan and Balor of the Fomorians—had the power of healing. He could revive a dying man by giving him water.

"Fionn," said Diarmuid, "bring me water and save me from dying."

Fionn reluctantly went to a nearby river and brought back water, but he remembered Gráinne and dropped it. Again Diarmuid pleaded with him, and again Fionn got water and dropped it. Finally, the rest of the Fianna threatened to kill him if he didn't bring water to Diarmuid. Fionn did so, but by that time Diarmuid was dead.

They brought his body back to Tara, but on the way Aengus saw them and took the body into the Brú, where he kept the spirit in the body for a few days so they could carry on a conversation. But after that, Aengus had to let the spirit go, and Diarmuid was dead forever.

Some say that Gráinne married Fionn in the end.

How Fionn Got His Gray Hair

The Slieve Cuilinn in this story is Slieve Gullion in South Armagh. The Sidhe woman Miluchradh is the Cailleach Bhéarra, who is associated with the tale of "The Hill of the Hag." Cuilinn is the same Culann from whom Cúchulainn took his name, "Hound of Culann," and Cuailgne is the Carlingford Peninsula east of Dundalk, County Louth—the Cooley of "The Cattle Raid of Cooley," the great epic the *Táin*.

The following story is a condensed form of "The Hunt of Slieve Cuilinn" found in Lady Gregory's book *Gods and Fighting Men* (1904).

Finn was one time out on the green of Almhuin, and he saw what had the appearance of a gray fawn running across the plain. He called and whistled to his hounds then, but neither hound nor man heard him or came to him, but only Bran and Sceolan. He set them after the fawn, and near as they kept to her, he himself kept nearer to them, till at last they reached Slieve Cuilinn, in the province of Ulster.

But they were no sooner at the hill than the fawn vanished from them, and they did not know where she was gone, and Finn went looking for her eastward, and the two hounds went towards the west.

It was not long till Finn came to a lake, and there was sitting on the brink of it a young girl, the most beautiful he had ever seen, having hair of the color of gold, and a skin as white as lime, and eyes like the stars in time of frost; but she seemed to be some way sorrowful and downhearted.

"What is it ails you, woman of the white hands?" said Finn, "and is there any help I can give you?"

"It is what I am fretting after," she said, "a ring of red gold I lost off my finger in the lake. And I put you under bonds, Finn of the Fianna, to bring it back to me out of the lake."

With that Finn stripped off his clothes and went into the lake at the bidding of the woman, and he went three times round the whole lake and did not leave any part of it without searching, till he brought back the ring. He handed it up to her then out of the water, and no sooner had he done that than she gave a leap into the water and vanished.

Cairn on summit of Slieve Gullion, County Armagh. This passage tomb is called Cailleach Bhéarra's House. The Cailleach, the wise old woman aspect of the Mother Goddess, is also associated with the passage tomb on Sliabh na Cailli known as the Witch's Cave and Ollamh Fodhla's Tomb.

And when Finn came up on the bank of the lake, he could not so much as reach to where his clothes were; for on the moment he, the head and leader of the Fianna of Ireland, was but a gray old man, weak and withered.

Bran and Sceolan came up to him then, but they did not know him, and they went on round the lake, searching after their master.

Caoilte and the rest of the chief men of the Fianna set out then looking for Finn, and at last they came to Slieve Cuilinn, and there they saw a withered old man sitting beside the lake, and they thought him to be a fisherman.

"Tell us, old man," said Caoilte, "did you see a fawn go by, and two hounds after her, and a tall fair-faced man along with them?"

"I did see them," he said, "and it is not long since they left me."

"Tell us where are they now," demanded Caoilte.

But Finn made no answer. For he had not the courage to say to them that he himself was Finn their leader, being as he was an ailing down-hearted old man, without leaping, without running, without walking, gray and sorrowful.

Caoilte took out his sword from the sheath then, and he said: "It is short till you will have the knowledge of death unless you will tell us what happened those three."

Then Finn told them the whole story. And when they knew it was Finn that was in it, they gave three loud sorrowful cries. And to the lake they gave the name of *Loch Doghra*, the "Lake of Sorrow."

And as to Finn, they asked him was there any cure to be found for him.

"There is," he said, "for I know well the enchantment was put on me by a woman of the Sidhe, Miluchradh, daughter of Cuilinn, through jealousy of her sister Aine. And bring me to the hill that belongs to Cuilinn of Cuailgne, for he is the only one can give me my shape again."

They came around him then, raised him up gently on their shields, and brought him on their shoulders to the hill of the Sidhe in Cuailgne.

Cuilinn of Cuailgne, that some say was Manannan son of Lir, came out of the hill holding in his hand a vessel of red gold, and he gave the vessel into Finn's hand. And no sooner did Finn drink what was in the vessel than his own shape and his appearance came back to him. But only his hair, that used to be so fair and so beautiful, like the hair of a woman, never got its own color again, for the lake that Cuilinn's daughter had made for Finn would have turned all the men of the whole world gray, if they had gone into it.

And when Finn had drunk all that was in the vessel, it slipped from his hand, and he saw it no more. But in the place where it went into the earth, a tree grew up, and any one who would look at the branches of the tree in the morning, fasting, would have knowledge of all that was to happen on that day.

Loch Doghra, the "Lake of Sorrow," on Slieve Gullion, County Armagh. This dark lake where Fionn got his gray hair is also called Cailleach Bhéarra's Lough.

That, now, is the way Finn came by his gray hair, through the jealousy of Miluchradh of the Sidhe, because he had not given his love to her, but to her sister Aine.

Fionn and the Scottish Giant
The Origin of the Giant's Causeway

By the 19th century, the English-speaking (and largely anti-Irish) landlord class in Ireland had discovered Fionn mac Cumhaill and changed him from a hero into an absurd comic figure. He became "our renowned Hibernian Hercules, the great and glorious Fin M'Coul." (The spelling of his name varies according to source and period.)

The most enduring of the burlesque literary tales of that period, "A Legend of Knockmany" (1845) by William Carleton is widely anthologized in variant forms. Unfortunately, it is the only "Finn McCool" piece in the repertoires of some non-Irish storytellers. My version below includes excerpts from Carleton's tale as it appears in Joseph Jacobs's *Celtic Fairy Tales* (1892).

Finn McCool was 27 feet tall. This is deduced from the size of a cast-off shoe of his that you can still see where he left it on the beach at the Giant's Causeway on the North Antrim coast. (It's really a large stone that looks remarkably like a shoe.) Finn built the Causeway so that he could travel to Scotland, but then he learned that a Scottish giant, Cucullin, planned to cross the Causeway to Ireland.

> Undoubtedly he had given every giant in Ireland a considerable beating, barring Finn M'Coul himself; and he swore that he would never rest, night or day, winter or summer, till he would serve Finn with the same sauce, if he could catch him. However, the short and long of it was, with reverence be it spoken, that Finn heard Cucullin was coming to the Causeway to have a trial of strength with him; and he was seized with a very warm and sudden fit of affection for his wife, poor woman, leading a very lonely, uncomfortable life of it in his absence.

Finn, watching from his home on Knockmany in County Tyrone, saw Cucullin striding across the Causeway and realized that, big as Finn was, he would be no match for the Scot. He had heard that the giant's strength lay in the middle finger of his right hand, and that without it he was no stronger than an ordinary man, but this was no use to Finn if he couldn't get near that finger before he was slaughtered.

The Giant's Causeway, County Antrim. Declared a World Heritage Site in 1986, the Causeway can claim a long geological and mythological history. The nearly 40,000 basaltic columns, mostly hexagonal, were formed by the cooling lava of a long-extinct volcano. The name in Irish, Clochán na bhFomórach, "The Stepping Stones of the Fomorians," attributes its construction to the dreaded Fomorians of prehistory, but more recent folklore tells how Fionn mac Cumhaill built it to challenge a Scottish giant.

"Oonagh," said he to his wife, "can you do nothing for me? Where's all your invention? How am I to fight this man-mountain, this huge cross between an earthquake and a thunderbolt?"

"Be easy, Finn," replied Oonagh. "Leave him to me, and do just as I bid you."

She sent round to the neighbors and borrowed one-and-twenty iron griddles, which she took and kneaded into the hearts of one-and-twenty cakes of bread, and these she baked on the fire in the usual way, setting them aside in the cupboard according as they were done. She then put down a large pot of new milk, which she made into curds and whey.

Oonagh dressed Finn in baby clothes and told him to lie in a boat that was done up to look like a cradle. When Cucullin arrived looking for Finn, Oonagh said he was not at home and invited the giant to make himself comfortable while she set the cakes on the table and put on the kettle to make a pot of tea.

"But first," she said, "I need a bit more water for the tea. Would you ever be so kind as to squeeze a couple of stones for me?"

"Squeeze stones for water?" said Cucullin, perplexed.

"Yes. That's what Finn always does when he's at home. He hasn't finished sinking the well yet." She pointed to a volcano-like crater in the top of the mountain.

Cucullin picked up a stone and squeezed it until it was nothing but dust, but no water came out. Finn, watching from the cradle, got a bit nervous when he saw this.

"Never mind, you poor man," said Oonagh. "You're probably tired from your long journey."

She handed a lump of curds to Finn in the cradle. Finn squeezed the curds, and Cucullin watched in amazement as the water trickled out.

"Ah, look," she said. "The wind is coming in the door. As Finn's away, would you ever be so kind as to pick up the house and turn it around? That's what Finn always does when the wind shifts."

If Cucullin was surprised at this, he made no comment, and with a great effort he managed to turn the house around. When Finn, lying quiet in his cradle, saw this, something happened that made him wish he was wearing a diaper. Cucullin was ready for refreshment when he finished the job, and he bit eagerly into one of the cakes with a griddle in the center that Oonagh had set out.

"Blood and fury!" he shouted. "How is this? Here are two of my teeth out! What kind of bread is this you gave me?"

"What's the matter?" said Oonagh coolly.

"Matter?" shouted the other again, "why, here are the two best teeth in my head gone."

"Why," said she, "that's Finn's bread, the only bread he ever eats when at home; but, indeed, I forgot to tell you that nobody can eat it but himself, and that child in the cradle there."

Finn was happily eating a cake that had no griddle in it.

"I'd dearly like to see the teeth of a child that can eat those cakes," said Cucullin.

And he went to the cradle and stuck the middle finger of his right hand into Finn's mouth. Finn bit it off, and the giant suddenly lost all his strength and a great deal more, for something happened to him that made him wish he was wearing a diaper. He took his leave with more speed than grace and hastened back to Scotland. He tore up the Causeway as he went so that Finn couldn't follow him, leaving the Ireland end of it in the ruined condition you can see now.

Fionn and the Battle of Gabhra A.D. 284
The End of the Fianna

Some say that this battle took place at Garristown in County Meath, where a large mound is said to be the burial place of Oscar. Others say it was at the Hill of Skreen (also called *Achaill*) near Tara. Both are probably correct, as the two sites are only seven miles apart and it was a major battle, and an alternative name of the battle is the Battle of Gabhra Achaill. The composition of the opposing sides reflected the Battle of Cnucha, in which Fionn's father, Cumhaill, was killed. For the Clan Morna took sides with Cairbre, who was now the high king, just as they had sided with his great-grandfather Conn against Cumhaill and his clan some 150 years previously.

The immediate cause of the battle was that Cairbre's daughter was given in marriage to a prince without first refusal or financial compensation being offered to the Fianna, as they felt was their right. But Aideen's rejection of Cairbre and her marriage to Oscar (see "Aideen and Oscar") was surely a contributing factor, as well as the death of Cairbre's three sons in the Battle of Cnámros, when the Fianna were allied with the Leinstermen against him.

Strong words were exchanged between Oscar and Cairbre, until Cairbre said:

> "I will put my spear of the seven spells out through your body."
> "And I give my word against that," said Oscar, "I will put my spear of the nine spells between the meeting of your hair and beard."

And it was at the hill of Gabhra the two armies met. And there were twenty men with the King of Ireland for every man that was with Fionn.

It was a very hard battle that was fought that day. There were great deeds done on both sides, and there never was a greater battle fought in Ireland than that one.

And as to Oscar, it would be hard to tell all he killed on that day: five score of the Sons of the Gael, and five score fighting men from the Country of Snow, and seven score of the Men of Green Swords that never went a step backward, and four hundred from the Country of the Lion, and five score of the sons of kings. And the shame was for the King of Ireland.

But as to Oscar himself, that began the day so swift and so strong, at the last he was like leaves on a strong wind, or like an aspen tree that is falling. But when he saw the High King near him, he made for him like a wave breaking on the strand; and the King saw him coming, and shook his greedy spear, and made a cast of it, and it went through his body and brought him down on his right knee, and that was the first grief of the Fianna.

But Oscar himself was no way daunted, but he made a cast of his spear of the nine spells that went into the High King at the meeting of the hair and the beard, and gave him his death. When the men nearest to the High King saw that, they put the King's helmet up on a pillar, the way his people would think he was living yet. But Oscar saw it, and he lifted a thin bit of a slabstone that was on the ground beside him, and he made a cast of it that broke the helmet where it was; and then he himself fell like a king.[5]

Hill of Skreen, County Meath. Ruins of the 15th century Church of Skreen (Scrín Cholmcille, or "Shrine of Colmcille") on the site of a ninth century monastery located on the Hill of Skreen east of the Hill of Tara. Saint Colmcille is said to have founded a church here in the 6th century, and his relics were kept here at one time, hence the name, Shrine.

There was not a hand's breadth of Oscar's body without a wound. As he lay dying, all the surviving warriors gathered around him, ignoring their own fallen sons and brothers, so loved was Oscar by everyone. Fionn was an old man at this time and did not take part in the combat.

When he arrived he said, "Oscar, you were wounded worse at the Battle of Ben Edar, and I gave you healing."

"There will be no healing for me this time," said Oscar, "since Cairbre put the spear of the seven spells through my body."

This account of the end of the Fianna comes down to us from the poet and historian of the Fianna, Oisín son of Fionn and father of Oscar. Oisín reports:

> "Fionn turned his back to us,
> And shed tears in abundance;
> Except for Oscar and Bran,
> He never shed tears for any one on earth."

That was the last battle the Fianna fought. There are three versions of what happened to Fionn after that. One is that he was killed in a battle with the Luaighne of Tara, a subject race. Another is that as an old man he died trying to leap across the River Boyne. But a persistent tradition has it that Fionn, like Red Hugh O'Donnell, lies sleeping in a cave with members of the Fianna and the Trumpet of the Fianna. Some day, a man will stumble upon the cave and blow three blasts on the Trumpet, and Fionn and the Fianna will awake and rise again as strong as ever.

Chapter 3

The Táin Bó Cuailnge

The Cattle Raid of Cooley and Its Hero, Cúchulainn

Maeve and Aillil's Pillow Talk

Eochaid Feidhleach ("Sighing"), high king of Ireland, had six daughters. One of them, Drebrenn, had three foster sisters, who, with their husbands, were turned into demon swine that ravaged Ireland until her sister Maeve broke the spell. Another, Clothra, seduced her three brothers and had one son fathered by all three, then had a son fathered by that son. She was pregnant by King Conor of Ulster, a previous husband of Maeve, when Maeve murdered her. Three of Eochaid's sons rebelled against him, and he had to kill them in self-defense. Little wonder he was called "Sighing."

His most notorious daughter, Maeve, queen of Connacht, described herself as "the noblest and seemliest" of the six. The Christian scribe who wrote this entry in the *Annals of Clonmacnoise* viewed her in a different light.

> "But the lady Maeve was of greater report than the rest because of her great boldness, beauty, and stout manliness in giving of battles, insatiable lust.
>
> "Her father allowed for her portion the province of Connaught, and she being thereof possessed grew so insolent and shameless that she made an oath never to marry with anyone whatsoever that would be stained with any of these three defects and imperfections as she accounted them, namely jealousy for any lechery that she should commit, with unmanliness or imbecility, so as the party could not be so bold as to undertake any adventure whatsoever were it never so difficult, and lastly she would never marry anyone that feared any man living." [6]

Maeve was married several times. Complications arising from her separation from Conor of Ulster contributed to the war described in the *Táin*. Maeve fell in love with her grandnephew, Aillil son of the king of Leinster,

Cooley Hills, Carlingford Peninsula near Dundalk, County Louth. The home of the Brown Bull of Cooley, owned by Dáire, king of Cooley.

and persuaded him to kill her then husband, Eochaid Dála, so that she could marry him. The story of the *Táin* begins with their "pillow talk."

Maeve and Aillil were lying in bed one morning, and Maeve said, "Isn't it a wonderful thing that you and I are equally wealthy. It would not be right for my husband to be wealthier than me, the Queen, and it would not be good for me to have more wealth than my husband."

They ordered their servants to bring in all their portable goods so that they could count them. Then they went outside to count their herds of cattle and horses and flocks of sheep. Among Aillil's cattle was one of the two greatest bulls in Ireland at that time, the Whitehorned.

When the counting was finished, Maeve said, "And besides all that, I have the Whitehorned Bull."

Aillil said, "You used to, but he refused to stay in a herd owned by a woman, so he has joined my herd."

This was a problem. They were not equal in wealth unless Maeve had the other outstanding bull, the Brown Bull of Cooley. This bull belonged to Dáire, king of Cooley, the present Carlingford Peninsula, then part of Ulster. Maeve sent messengers to Dáire to ask him to lend her the Brown Bull in exchange for land and cattle—and "my own closest intimacy," if he brought it in person—and he agreed. In fact, he shook with such pleasure that the cushions he was sitting on burst.

Maeve's messengers celebrated the good news with an unwise amount of drink, and they boasted, "It's a good thing Dáire agreed to lend the bull to Maeve, otherwise she would have taken it."

Dáire's servants overheard this and reported it to Dáire. He got angry and changed his mind.

When the messengers reported this to Maeve, she said, predictably, "Right. I'll take it."

Maeve called in political favors and added to her own Connacht warriors those of Munster and Leinster and the band of Ulster exiles led by the former Ulster king, Fergus mac Roich ("Manly Strength son of Big Horse").

Why was the former King of Ulster helping Maeve of Connacht invade Ulster? The next story, "The Tragic Death of the Sons of Uisliu," one of the Three Sorrowful Tales of Ireland, explains why.

The Tragic Death of the Sons of Uisliu
The Deirdre Story

Neasa was a headstrong and ambitious young woman.

One day at Emain Macha, the royal palace of Ulster, she met with the druid Cathbad and asked him, "What is today a good day for?"

"Today is a good day to beget a king," said Cathbad.

"Come with me, Cathbad," said Neasa, "and let's see what happens."

Nine months later, Neasa gave birth to a son, Conor. Fergus mac Roich, King of Ulster, wanted to marry Neasa.

Neasa agreed on condition that Fergus allow Conor to be king for a year, so that his sons could say that they were sons of a king. Fergus agreed.

During the year of Conor's reign, Neasa and Conor lavishly bestowed gifts on the nobles of Ulster, plundering not only their own resources but also the treasury of Ulster itself.

Navan Fort, near Armagh City, County Armagh. Navan Fort is the modern name of Emain Macha, the seat of the kings of Ulster from 660 B.C. until 330 A.D., when it was ceremoniously filled with stones, burned, and covered over with earth. The Red Branch Hall stood next to the king's palace.

At the end of the year, when Fergus asked for his crown back, the nobles said, "Fergus, we have decided that we prefer Conor as king, if you don't mind."

They said it in such a way that Fergus knew it didn't matter if he did mind, so he contented himself with the post of arms master to the Boy Troop.

Conor and his warriors, the Knights of the Red Branch, were attending a feast at the house of Fedlimid the poet, when an unearthly shriek echoed through the house. The warriors sprang to their weapons. Conor said to the druid Cathbad, "What was that noise?"

Cathbad said, "That is the cry of the girl-child in the womb of Fedlimid's wife. She will bring red grief to the Red Branch warriors, brother will fight brother, and her name will be *Deirdre* ['Grief']."

"Let's kill her as soon as she is born," said the brave warriors, "and prevent this trouble."

"No," said Conor. "She will be raised apart from men, and when she is of age, I will marry her myself."

Deirdre was raised in a secret place in the forest with only Levorcham, a woman poet, as her companion. She never saw a man except Conor, and she thought all men were old and gray.

One night, when she was 18, she had a vision in which appeared a handsome young man with white skin, red lips, and black hair, and she fell immediately in love with him. At the same time, Naoise, a Red Branch knight who had been hunting in the forest and was camping near Deirdre's hideaway, had a vision of a beautiful young woman. The following day, they happened to meet, and each recognized in the other the person in their vision.

They eloped, were chased all over Ireland by Conor, and found refuge in Scotland for ten years. Naoise's Red Branch comrades persuaded—they thought—Conor to forgive Deirdre and Naoise and allow them to return to Ireland. Conor sent Fergus to accompany them under his guarantee of safety.

Deirdre had a foreboding and pleaded with Naoise not to trust Conor, but Naoise insisted that they would be safe with Fergus.

However, as soon as they landed at Ballycastle in County Antrim, Conor used a binding vow of Fergus's not to refuse an invitation to a feast. He had bribed the local lord, Barach, to invite Fergus to a feast. Conor had made Fergus promise that Deirdre and Naoise would come to Emain Macha immediately on landing in Ireland, so Fergus had to leave Deirdre and Naoise in the care of his sons.

Deirdre said, "If Conor invites us to eat with him in the king's palace, we will be safe, because he can't kill us once he has given us hospitality. But if he sends us directly to the Red Branch Hall, I'm afraid there will be red slaughter."

And that is exactly what happened.

As Deirdre and Naoise sat playing fidchell (a board game like chess) after their dinner in the Red Branch Hall, Conor sent Levorcham to look at Deirdre and describe her. Levorcham saw that Deirdre was more beautiful than ever, but she didn't trust Conor.

She reported: "Ach, the poor girl. She's been living rough these past ten years, and she's lost all her beauty. She looks twice her age."

Conor didn't trust Levorcham and sent a servant. The servant climbed a ladder and peeked through a window at Deirdre and Naoise. Naoise saw him and threw a fidchell piece at him, taking out an eye.

The servant reported to Conor: "Naoise took out one of my eyes with a fidchell piece, but I would gladly give the other eye to look at Deirdre again. In the full bloom of maturity, she is the most beautiful woman in the world."

That sealed their fate. Conor ordered the Red Branch to attack the hall and kill Naoise and bring Deirdre to him.

This caused a revolt among the warriors, and they fought one another, bringing red slaughter to the Red Branch. Eventually, Eoghan mac Dubhtacht killed Naoise, and Conor took Deirdre to live with him for a year.

During that time, Deirdre never looked up or smiled.

At the end of the year, Conor said to her, "Besides me, who do you hate most in the world?"

"Eoghan mac Dubhtacht."

"Right," said Conor. "You're going to spend the next year with Eoghan."

Conor was taking Deirdre, tied behind him in his chariot, to Eoghan. As they passed along the side of a cliff, Deirdre saw a projecting rock ahead, and when the chariot reached that spot, she leaned out of the chariot and dashed her head against the rock so that she died.

When Fergus returned to Emain Macha from Barach's feast and found out how his guarantee had been violated, he burned the royal palace and went with his followers to Maeve in Connacht.

He was given a warm welcome. It was said of Maeve that it took 30 men a day to satisfy her—or Fergus once.

"Maeve had three in an hour, they say."—*from W. B. Yeats,* The Death of Cuchulain *(1939)*

The Curse of Macha

As soon as Maeve's combined army, the "men of Ireland," set off in the direction of the Ulster border, all the men of Ulster suddenly fell sick and took to their beds, weak as a woman in childbirth. This was because of the Curse of Macha.

Cruinniuc, an Ulster lord, was sitting in front of his house one day, when he saw a beautiful woman walking up the road in his direction, and he thought it a pity that he had lived all his life so far without knowing her. To his surprise, she turned off the road and walked up his front path, passed him without a word, went into the house, into the kitchen, and prepared dinner. He had never eaten such a kingly meal prepared by so queenly a woman. After dinner, she climbed into his bed, nature took its course, and after nine months, she was ready to give birth.

Saint Patrick's Cathedral (Protestant), Armagh, County Armagh. The Protestant cathedral, a 19th century restoration of a 13th century building, stands on one of the two heights in Armagh and faces the Catholic cathedral across the city. Brian Boru, the high king who broke the power of the Norsemen in 1014, is said to be buried in the churchyard.

Cruinniuc had learned that her name was Macha, and that she loved to run. She could run faster than any animal, even the nimblest deer or speediest horse, and by that he knew that she was not from this world.

There was a fair at Ulster's royal seat, soon to be called Emain Macha, and Cruinniuc went to partake in the festivities, watch the horseracing, and celebrate the imminent birth.

When King Conor's horse won the race, Cruinniuc, well into his cups, boasted loudly, "I have a wife at home who can run faster than Conor's horse."

Conor heard this and said, "Bring your wife here and prove that she can outrun my horse, or I'll have your head."

Cruinniuc sobered up quickly and went home and told Macha that she had to go to the fair and race against Conor's horse.

"But look at my belly," Macha said. "I can't run in my condition. It would be dangerous for both me and the baby."

"Let's go and show Conor your belly," said Cruinniuc, "and I'm sure he'll let you run the race after the baby is born."

When they appeared before Conor and asked for a postponement, Conor said, "No. You prove right now that you can run faster than my horse, or off with your husband's head."

Macha turned to the Ulster warriors and pleaded, "Men of Ulster, make Conor change his mind. I can't run in my condition."

The men of Ulster turned their backs on her. She ran the race and beat Conor's horse, but as she crossed the finish line she fell down dying, and gave birth to twins. From this comes the name of the royal seat of Ulster: Emain Macha, the "Twins of Macha."

With her dying breath, she cursed the men of Ulster: "At the time of Ulster's greatest need and danger, all the men of Ulster will be as weak and sick as a woman in childbirth."

This is why the men of Ulster took to their beds as soon as Maeve's army began its march toward their border.

The modern city of Armagh is named after this or another Macha: *Ard Macha*, the "Height of Macha." Some say the Twins of Macha are the two hills in the city, one topped by the Roman Catholic cathedral and the other by the Church of Ireland cathedral. (Saint Patrick made Armagh the seat of the Christian Church.) Others identify the Twins as the two mounds at Navan Fort, about two miles west of the city, which were the palace of the king and the headquarters of the Red Branch warriors.

The Macha in this story merges two mythological personages: a continental Celtic horse goddess named Epona, and the Macha who forms the trinity of Irish battle goddesses with the Mórrígan and Badhbh. Another very different story derives the name from an Ulster warrior queen called Macha, who reigned in the third (or sixth, according to one source) century B.C. as the 76th monarch of Ireland.

Saint Patrick's Cathedral (Catholic), Armagh, County Armagh. Saint Patrick chose Armagh City as the seat of the Christian Church in Ireland in A.D. 445. Two cathedrals, one Catholic and the other Protestant, occupy the two prominent heights in the city. The gothic-style Catholic cathedral was completed in 1873.

The Birth of Cúchulainn

With the men of Ulster powerless to resist, it was left to Cúchulainn to defend the kingdom against Maeve's invasion. Still officially a boy at the age of 17 and not completely human—as the son of Lugh of the Tuatha Dé Danaan—Cúchulainn was not affected by Macha's curse. Stories of his birth, life, and death are entwined with the great epic. His original name was Sétanta.

Dechtire was the sister of King Conor of Ulster. She married Sualtam, a Red Branch knight, whose home was the border post at Dún Dealgan, a fortified hill west of Dundalk, County Louth. On her wedding night, she had a vision in which a strange man lay with her. When she awoke, the man was standing next to her bed. He told her he was Lugh Lámfhada ("of the Long Arm") and that she would bear his son.

The following morning, Dechtire and her fifty handmaidens were missing. Conor and the Red Branch warriors searched throughout Ireland, and at the end of nine months stopped for the night at Newgrange, where they were invited by the servants to have dinner.

After the meal, Conor said to one of the servants, "We haven't met our host and hostess yet. We would like to give them our thanks for the hospitality."

The servant said, "Our mistress is in bed giving birth just now. You can see her in the morning."

When Conor went to visit the lady of the house next morning, who did she turn out to be but his sister, Dechtire. After the obvious questions had been asked and answered, Dechtire and her son went to live at Dún Dealgan. Sualtam drops out of the story until he appears briefly in the *Táin*. Dechtire named her son Sétanta. How he got the name Cúchulainn is told in the story "How Cúchulainn Got His Name."

On the night Sétanta was born, two colts were foaled that would later become his chariot horses. They were the Gray of Macha and the Black Sainglain.

Dún Dealgan, Dundalk, County Louth. Dún Dealgan ("Dealgan's Fort") was the childhood home and later the fortified base of Cúchulainn, the hero of the epic Táin Bó Cuailnge, *the Cattle Raid of Cooley. While the men of Ulster were incapacitated by the Curse of Macha, he single-handedly resisted the invasion of Ulster by Queen Maeve.*

Sétanta Goes to Emain Macha

When Sétanta was five years old, he noticed a group of warriors heading north past Dún Dealgan toward Emain Macha, about 25 miles (40 km) away.

"Who are those warriors?" he asked his mother.
"They're Red Branch knights."
"Where are they going?"
"To Emain Macha, to be with my brother, King Conor."
"I want to be a Red Branch knight."
"Yes, dear. When you grow up."
"No, I want to be a Red Branch knight now. I'm going to Emain Macha."

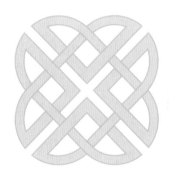

And off he went, taking nothing with him but his hurley and sliotar and javelin. (The *hurley* is the bat, and the *sliotar* is the ball, about the size of a tennis ball but hard like a baseball, used in the still popular Gaelic game of hurling.) He amused himself along the road by batting the sliotar into the air with the hurley, tossing the hurley and javelin after it, and catching all three before they hit the ground.

When he arrived at the green in front of the king's palace at Emain Macha, he saw the Boy Troop playing hurling. Seeing this as an opportunity to become acquainted with his contemporaries, he dashed in among them, knocked them down and took the sliotar away from them, and scored a goal. Boys were lying all over the hurling pitch with broken and bleeding heads and noses, crying and screaming. Fergus mac Roich, arms master to the Boy Troop, came out of the palace to see what was going on.

"This boy knocked us down and took the sliotar away from us," they complained. "And what's more, he didn't even ask for our protection as a stranger."

"Is that true, boy?" Fergus asked Sétanta.

"Yes. I didn't know I was supposed to ask for their protection. But look at them. They should have asked for *my* protection."

"Well, there may be something in that, but you did violate our custom of asking protection when you arrive as a stranger. What is your name, and who are your people?"

"I'm Sétanta. My mother is Dechtire, sister of King Conor."

"Well, Sétanta, welcome to Emain Macha. I haven't seen you since you were born. I'm one of your foster fathers, and the great Conall Cearnach is your foster brother. Come in to the palace and meet your Uncle Conor."

How Cúchulainn Got His Name

One day when Sétanta was seven years old, Conor and the Red Branch knights were invited to a feast at the house of the smith Culann. As they set off, Conor stopped at the hurling pitch where Sétanta was playing with the Boy Troop.

"Sétanta," said Conor, "come with us to Culann's house for a feast."

"I'm busy playing hurling, but you go ahead and I'll follow your chariot tracks later."

When the match was over, Sétanta followed the tracks of Conor and the warriors, batting the sliotar into the air and throwing the hurley after it and catching both before they hit the ground. Meanwhile, the feast was in full swing with much eating and drinking and more drink-

Cooley Hills, Carlingford Peninsula near Dundalk, County Louth. Home of the Brown Bull of Cooley, which was owned by Dáire, king of Cooley, the present Carlingford Peninsula. Culann, who appears in "How Fionn Got His Gray Hair" (pp. 45-47), also made his home here.

ing. As the evening grew darker, Culann said to Conor, "Are all of your people here now?"

Forgetting about Sétanta, Conor said, "Yes. Why do you ask?"

"It's getting dark, and I'm going to let my guard dog loose. He'll kill anyone who approaches the house at night, so I wanted to know if you were expecting more of your people."

"No," said Conor. "We're all here. You can let the dog out."

Some say that this hound was the Brown Whelp of the infamous bitch Luch Donn ("Brown Mouse"), who devastated Ulster until the hero Celtchair killed her. Luch Donn's Speckled Whelp was the cause of the slaughter that is the subject of another Ulster tale, "Mac Dathó's Pig." The blood of the Black Whelp was so poisonous that Celtchair died after touching a drop of it. Others say that the hound that guarded Culann's house at this time was not that Brown Whelp but one that came from Spain. In any case, he had the strength of a hundred hounds, and it took three men with three chains each to hold him.

Sétanta arrived at Culann's house, still batting the sliotar into the air and tossing the hurley after it and catching both before they hit the ground. The hound went for him. The men in the house heard the commotion and looked out the windows, aghast. They were helpless to prevent the hound attacking little Sétanta. But Sétanta calmly tossed the sliotar into the air, batted it with the hurley, and drove it into the hound's mouth, down its throat, through the body and out the other end, killing the animal.

The men came out of the house and gathered around Sétanta, greatly relieved that he had escaped unharmed.

Culann, however, complained, "It took me a year to raise and train that hound to protect my house. What am I going to do for a guard dog until I can raise and train another one?"

Sétanta said, "Since I killed your hound, I will be your guard dog for the next year. I will be the Hound of Culann."

"Hound of Culann" in Irish is *Cú Chulainn*, and that is how Cúchulainn got his name.

Cúchulainn's Single Combat with Ferdia

The Irish name of Ardee, County Louth, is *Ath Fhirdia*, the "Ford of Ferdia." Local tradition says that Cúchulainn and Ferdia's single combat took place at the ford on the River Dee, a five-minute walk west of the bridge through a riverside park at the south end of the town. A standing stone erected by Maeve and Aillil marks the site. A modern bronze sculpture of the two warriors stands in a public parking lot near the bridge. This episode is one of the longest, best known, and most tragic and poetic in the *Táin*. The prose text frequently breaks off to accommodate repetitions in formal verse of the more emotional dialogues.

Cúchulainn's Single Combat with Ferdia, *from Desmond Kinney's 1974 glass and ceramic mosaic mural on the side of the Northern Ireland Tourist Board Office, Nassau Street, Dublin.*

This recent statue in Ardee, County Louth, shows Cúchulainn carrying the dead body of his best friend, Ferdia. Cúchulainn was forced to fight Ferdia in single combat at the nearby ford.

At the age of seventeen, shortly before he defended Ulster against Maeve's invasion, Cúchulainn attended a warriors' finishing school run by the woman warrior Scáthach on the Isle of Skye. There he met Ferdia, a horn-skinned Fir Bolg from Connacht. Evenly matched in battle skills, the two became best friends. The only advantage Cúchulainn had over Ferdia was the Gae Bolga, a unique mysterious weapon given to him by Scáthach. It was a spring-loaded javelin launched by the foot from the surface of the water. When it struck the opponent in the stomach, thirty barbed points sprang from its head, penetrating throughout the body. The only way to remove it was to cut the body apart.

As Maeve's army neared the Ulster border, Cúchulainn was killing a hundred warriors a day. To stem her losses, Maeve proposed that she send champions to engage in single combat with Cúchulainn. He agreed, hoping to stall until the Ulstermen could recover from their pangs, on the condition that Maeve's army would remain inactive during the fights.

He greeted the first contender with the timeless challenge: "What are you looking at?"

Not surprisingly, Cúchulainn defeated all of Maeve's champions, even when she cheated by sending six at a time.

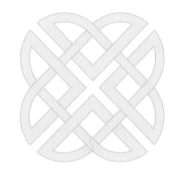

It soon became difficult, then impossible, for her to find volunteers, although she offered the incentives of wealth, land, and her daughter Finnabair. Finally, there was only one Connacht warrior left alive with a chance of defeating Cúchulainn—Ferdia. Maeve sent messengers to Ferdia, but he ignored them. She sent poets and satirists to shame him and to curse him with death if he did not come within nine days, and so he arrived reluctantly at Maeve's camp. He was plied with drink and food, Finnabair gave him three kisses for every cup of wine and served him sweet apples from her cleavage, and whatever Maeve had offered to the other champions was multiplied many times over for Ferdia and his descendants—all tax-free to the end of time.

To top it off, Maeve extended an invitation to "my friendly thighs." Ferdia turned her down, but Maeve was an expert manipulator of fragile male pride.

"So, it's true what Cúchulainn said about you," she said.

"What did he say?"

"That he wouldn't consider it one of his greatest deeds to defeat you," she lied. "I suppose he was right, and you're only a coward."

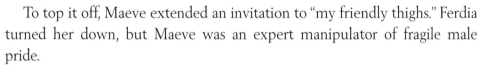

Ferdia and Cúchulainn met at the ford at Ardee and alternately praised and insulted each other, recalled and renounced their friendship, and exchanged boasts and threats.

"Your coming is welcome, Cúchulainn."

"Once I trusted your welcome, but no more. It would be more appropriate for me to welcome you, because you have come to my territory."

"When we were with Scáthach, you were my servant. You used to sharpen my spears and make my bed."

"That is true. I was young then, but now there is no warrior in the world I cannot defeat."

"Little Hound, why do you come to fight with a mighty champion?

Your flesh will be blood-red above the steam of your horses."

"I will attack you with sharp weapons and thrust you under the water."

"You have the heart of a little bird."

"When we were with Scáthach, we fought side by side. You were my beloved comrade. Your death will be sad to me."

"Before the cock crows tomorrow, Cúchulainn, your head will be displayed on a spike."

As the first to reach the ford, Ferdia had the choice of weapons for the first day. They fought with javelins and blades until midday without either wounding the other, so good were their defenses.

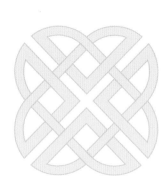

From noon to nightfall they cast spears at each other, and both were wounded. At the end of the day, they gave their weapons to their charioteers and put their arms around each other's neck and kissed. That night, they shared food and healing herbs so that no one could say that one took advantage of the other because of a lack of care.

For the second day, Cúchulainn chose spear thrusting from chariots as the form of combat. Birds could have flown through the gaping wounds they inflicted on each other from dawn to dusk. Again they embraced and kissed, and their charioteers spent the night at one campfire, their horses in one paddock. Doctors had to use spells and charms as well as bandages to staunch the blood that flowed from their injuries. They sent food to each other from their beds on opposite sides of the river. Ferdia appeared gloomy the following morning.

"Ferdia, you are doomed," said Cúchulainn, "for you fight your foster brother at the behest of a woman. You are the cause of all that will happen. The man has not been born for whom I would wish to harm you."

"It is not you but Maeve who has betrayed us. You will have victory."

"My heart is heavy. This is not an equal fight."

Ferdia chose to use long swords. The chunks of flesh they hacked out of each other's bodies were the size of a baby's head. That night their charioteers did not share a campfire, and their horses were paddocked separately.

On the morning of the fourth day, Ferdia rose early and tied a millstone in front of his belly and an iron apron over the stone for fear of the Gae Bolga. The choice of weapons was Cúchulainn's, and he said that all weapons would be allowed.

Such was the ferocity of their encounter that their spears bent, their shields split, goblins of the earth and demons of the air screamed, the river was forced from its bed, the horses of Maeve's army panicked and broke loose, and women and children went mad.

At last, Ferdia broke through Cúchulainn's guard and plunged his sword into his chest, wounding him severely. Desperate, Cúchulainn called to his charioteer to float the Gae Bolga along the surface of the water to him. When Ferdia heard that, he lowered the stone and the iron apron to protect his belly. Cúchulainn thrust his short spear over Ferdia's guard and ran it through his body. When Ferdia raised the stone and apron too late, Cúchulainn launched the Gae Bolga upward with his right foot into Ferdia's unprotected belly.

River Dee, Ardee, County Louth

It was all over, except for a long formal lament by Cúchulainn in 42 stanzas, of which this is one:

"All was merely game and sport
Till Ferdia fought me at the ford.
Beloved Ferdia would survive,
I thought, long after I had died.
Who was a mountain yesterday
Today is nothing but a shade."
—*from the* Book of Leinster

The Death of Cúchulainn

Maeve harbored deep resentment at the way Cúchulainn had humiliated her during the invasion of Ulster, even though she eventually captured the Brown Bull.

Cúchulainn was involved in many adventures in the ten years following the *Táin*, and relatives of the victims of some of those adventures also held grudges, notably three sorceresses, whose father, Calatin, Cúchulainn had killed along with their 27 brothers. Lugaid son of Cú Roí and Erc son of Cairbre Niafer also longed to avenge the deaths of their fathers. Maeve sent the Daughters of Calatin to study the dark arts in graduate schools around Europe and as far away as Babylon. When they returned to Ireland, Maeve called them and Lugaid and Erc together to organize Cúchulainn's death.

She launched an attack on Ulster to lure Cúchulainn out.

Conor divined her purpose and ordered Cúchulainn to stay away from the front lines. Cúchulainn's famously unjealous wife, Emer, took him to the Silent Valley in the Mourne Mountains, where the sounds of battle could not penetrate, and surrounded him with his girlfriends and mistresses.

The Daughters of Calatin were not able to find him for some time, but eventually they spied his horses and chariot and began to ply their arts outside the house where he was staying. They magicked stacks of straw into the forms of warriors and raised the din of battle around the house. Emer and the other women managed to convince Cúchulainn

Clochafarmore ("Stone of the Big Man"), near Knockbridge, County Louth. According to local tradition, this is the pillar to which Cúchulainn tied himself after he received his fatal wound, so he would die standing facing his enemies. The field where it is located is still called the Field of Slaughter.

Gable Art, Shankill Road, Belfast. The Death of Cúchulainn depicted on the gable end of a house on Shankill Road, a Protestant street in Belfast. In the Republic this image represents the War of Independence from Britain, and in Protestant areas of the North, it is often seen in "gable art" as a symbol of Loyalist resistance to the prospect of a united Ireland. The example in this photo promotes the Loyalist paramilitary Ulster Defence Association. The Red Hand flag of Ulster flies above the image.

that it was trickery until the Daughters of Calatin imitated the sound of Conor's shield.

One of the properties of the shield was that it would scream for help when its owner was attacked. When Cúchulainn heard what he thought was a call to come to the aid of his king, he broke loose from the women, mounted his chariot, and with the faithful Laeg at the reins, drove toward where the battle seemed to be.

Several ill omens occurred in quick succession.

When he went to fasten his cloak, his brooch slipped and fell, stabbing him in the foot. One of his chariot horses, the Gray of Macha, refused to let himself be harnessed until Cúchulainn persuaded him. Then large red teardrops fell from the Gray's eyes and landed on Cúchulainn's foot.

He stopped to say farewell to his mother, Dechtire. She offered him a cup of white wine. But when he looked into the cup, the wine had turned blood red.

He passed a Washer at the Ford, an Otherworld woman who makes a frequent appearance in Irish legend, who was washing clothes in a stream. The clothes resembled Cúchulainn's own and blood was running from them.

He encountered three old women, who offered him a piece of a dog they were roasting. It was *geis* (taboo) for him to eat dog meat because of his name, but to avoid offending the women he accepted the portion with his left hand. That hand immediately lost all its strength.

Cúchulainn and Laeg arrived at the site selected by Maeve for the sham battle. Pairs of men appeared to be engaged in single combat.

One man called to Cúchulainn, "Give me your spear."

The Death of Cúchulainn, *from Desmond Kinney's 1974 glass and ceramic mosaic mural on the side of the Northern Ireland Tourist Board Office, Nassau Street, Dublin.*

Mountains of Mourne, County Down. Cúchulainn's wife, Emer, concealed him in the Silent Valley in the Mourne Mountains to protect him from the magical machinations of the Daughters of Calatin.

Cúchulainn said, "I need it to defend Ulster."

"I'll put a curse on you if you don't give it to me."

"Take it then." Cúchulainn cast his spear at him, and it went through his head and the heads of eight men behind him.

Lugaid picked up the spear and said to the Daughters of Calatin, "What will happen if I throw this spear?"

"A king will die."

Lugaid threw the spear at Cúchulainn. It missed him but killed Laeg, the son of a king and a king among charioteers.

Cúchulainn took the reins and again charged into battle.

Another man called to him, "Cúchulainn, give me your spear."

Cúchulainn said, "I need it to defend Ulster."

"I'll put a curse on you if you don't give it to me."

"Take it then." Cúchulainn cast his spear at him, and it went through his head and the heads of eight men behind him. Erc picked up the spear and said to the Daughters of Calatin, "What will happen if I throw this spear?"

"A king will die."

Erc threw the spear at Cúchulainn. It missed him but mortally wounded the Gray of Macha, a king among horses. Cúchulainn cut the Gray out of the traces and charged once more into battle with the Black Sainglain.

A man called to Cúchulainn, "Give me your spear."

Cúchulainn said, "I need it to defend Ulster."

"I'll put a curse on you if you don't give it to me."

"Take it then." Cúchulainn cast his spear at him, and it went through his head and the heads of eight men behind him. Lugaid picked up the spear and said to the Daughters of Calatin, "What will happen if I throw this spear?"

"A king will die."

Lugaid threw the spear at Cúchulainn, and it struck him in the middle, spilling his intestines onto the floor of the chariot. Cúchulainn knew that the wound was fatal.

He gathered his intestines back into his body and said to his enemies, "Allow me to go down to that lake at the bottom of the field and wash the blood off myself before I die."

They stood back and allowed him to wash. Then he returned to the top of the field and tied himself to a tall standing stone with his belt, so that he would die standing and facing his enemies rather than lying down.

The mortally wounded Gray of Macha returned to fend off Cúchulainn's attackers with teeth and hooves until the hero light faded from his master's forehead and Badhbh, the battle goddess, landed on Cúchulainn's shoulder in the form of a raven.

Cúchulainn's death pillar stands in a field still known locally as the Field of Slaughter. It is signposted as Clochafarmore ("Stone of the Big Man") on the road to Knockbridge, about four miles (5.5 km) southwest of Dundalk, County Louth.

Chapter 4

Legends of Saints

Brigit, Saint and Goddess

The "goddess" Brigit (also Bridget, Brigid, Brighid) is the wife or three wives or the daughter or three daughters of the Dagda, chief of the Tuatha Dé Danaan. An aspect of the Mother Goddess, she is a patroness of three professions: art (especially poetry), healing (including fertility), and metal-working (specifically fire). Many of these goddess attributes have been assumed by the saint who bears her name and is seen by some people as an incarnation of the goddess. This has the effect of re-mythologizing the saint.

Saint Brigit (c. 439–524) is one of the three most prominent saints in Ireland, along with Patrick, whose shroud she wove, and Colmcille. Tradition says she is buried with them at Downpatrick in County Down. Miracles of healing, fire, and fertility are at the center of many of the legends about her.

Saint Brigit's father was a lord at Faughart, about two miles north of Dundalk, County Louth, where an earthen mound near a churchyard on Faughart Hill is locally said to be Brigit's birthplace. The ruins of the church mark the site of a church founded by Brigit, and the holy well in the grounds is frequently visited. Faughart Hill was the scene of many battles, legendary and historical, including two with Cúchulainn in the *Táin*. Edward, brother of the Scottish king Robert Bruce, was killed and buried there in 1318. A 19th century owner of the land reported turning up old swords and bullets when he plowed.

Brigit's father impregnated a household servant. When his wife discovered this, she ordered the pregnant woman out of the house. The servant, who was to be Brigit's mother, was given to a druid. Brigit was born in appropriately mythical circumstances: as her mother carried milk into the

house at sunrise and had one foot inside and the other on the threshold. When Brigit was three years old, a cloth caught fire and landed on her head. Her mother and the druid hastened to snatch the cloth away, but they found that neither Brigit nor the cloth showed burn marks.

When Brigit reached her teens, she returned to her father's home. Her nurse fell ill with a fever one day and had a craving for mead to quench her thirst. Unable to find mead, Brigit drew water from a well, and by the time she gave it to the nurse, it had turned to mead.

Saint Brigit's Shrine, Kildare, County Kildare.

Saint Brigit's Shrine at the foot of Faughart Hill, County Louth.

She was constantly in trouble for giving away food (a Mother Goddess attribute). Once, when a beggar came to the house, she gave him the last of the meat in the kitchen. When dinnertime came, she prayed to God to help her, and enough meat appeared miraculously to feed the household.

She was supposed to look after the sheep, but she spent her days in prayer and meditation. Her father decided to teach her a lesson about responsibility. He secretly locked away two sheep and then asked Brigit to count the animals in her care. Miraculously, they were all present.

She is always described as a great beauty. A young man with good family connections came courting, and her father was pressing her to accept his suit. Brigit took out one of her eyes and the suitor's ardor was suddenly cooled. In an alternative version, she prayed and God gave her a disfiguring eye infection. With that crisis over, Brigit's eye was healed. Many holy wells dedicated to Brigit are specifically for eye ailments.

During the ceremony when Brigit took her vows as a nun, she touched a wooden altar, and it burst into flame. Other versions tell of the wooden altar putting forth green leaves. Another account says that the bishop, "intoxicated with the grace of God," read the wrong ritual and mistakenly consecrated her a bishop.

Needing land to establish a monastery in Kildare Town, Brigit asked a local lord to donate some of his property.

He was unwilling, so he jokingly said, "I'll give you as much land as your cloak will cover."

Brigit laid her cloak on the ground, and it grew and began to spread and spread, until the lord said, "Stop it before it covers the whole country. I'll give you all the land you want."

A man asked her to do something to restore his wife's interest in sex. Brigit prayed, and the man returned, complaining that now his wife wouldn't leave him alone.

"You should be more careful what you ask for," was her reply.

As the territorial protector of Leinster, Brigit looked after the Leinster warriors when they fought against the kings of Tara. Even the great Saint Colmcille, protector of the Tara forces, backed down when he saw Brigit hovering over the Leinstermen in the Battle of Allen in A.D. 722.

Brigit was nursing a pagan lord who was ill, and as she sat next to his bed she was plaiting rushes from the floor into the form of a cross. The lord asked her what the cross represented, and she told him the story of Christ. He was so impressed he became a Christian.

That is the origin of the Brigit's Cross, an ancient sun and fire symbol, which is mounted fresh each year inside the doors of many Irish houses on Brigit's feast day, the first of February, which is also the official first day of spring in Ireland. It is said to be for good luck, but specifically it is meant to prevent accidental fires.

In Saint Brigit, ancient pagan and modern Irish Catholic minds meet amicably. Some Irish environmentalists have adopted her as their patron, and many present-day admirers pray to her as the latest incarnation of the goddess Brigit. A perpetual fire in Kildare Town in honor of the goddess, which had been continued in honor of the saint until the English extinguished it in the 16th century, was symbolically rekindled by the Roman Catholic Order of the Brigidine Sisters in 1993 as the "fire of love."

And as poetic muse, Brigit has inspired perhaps more legends than any other Irish saint, as well as a hymn by her kinsman Ultán, the 7th century saint, bishop, and poet, which begins:

"Christ has shown to Irish people
Miracles from Heaven sent
Through the virgin blessed with healing
For our health and betterment."[7]

Saint Colmcille

Born into the royal O'Neills too far down the line of succession for any hope of kingship, the man who came to be known as Saint Colmcille (A.D. 520–593) was educated as a poet and druid. Like many poet-druids of the time, he sensed the shifting of political winds and converted to Christianity. His birth name was Crimthann ("Fox"), which some commentators say suited him better than the name he changed it to: Colm ("Dove").

Both the documented historical facts of his life and the legends that have collected around him reveal a character alternately pious and irascible, even vicious at times, but strangely appealing.

He is called Colmcille ("Colm of the Churches") in Ireland and Western Scotland for the 365 churches he established, but *Columba*, Latin for "Dove," is the form of his name found on some Protestant churches in Ireland.

Colm is credited with founding a monastery at Derry in A.D. 546, although this is disputed. A few years later, he won a legal quarrel with his cousin, High King Diarmait mac Cerbaill, for which he was awarded the town of Kells in County Meath as compensation. He immediately turned it into a monastery, the boundaries of which are more or less indicated by the present-day wall around the Saint Columba church grounds. The only visible remains of the monastery are the high crosses, an 11th century round tower, and the 9th century "House of Colmcille," which is variously described as an oratory or a scriptorium (where manuscripts were written and transcribed).

In 560, Colm started a civil war. He had surreptitiously copied out a psalter belonging to his teacher, Finnen. When Finnen discovered this, he demanded that Colm hand over the copy. Colm refused, and the case was taken to King Diarmait for his judgment. Diarmait ruled in favor of Finnen, and in the process established the first copyright law in Ireland: "To every cow her calf, and to every book its copy."

This infuriated Colm, who was noted for his short temper.

He was also famous for granting his protection, even long after his death, and he had given his protection to a son of the king of Connacht. When Diarmait violated that protection by executing the boy for murder, Colm gathered warriors to fight against Diarmait. Three thousand of Diarmait's warriors were killed in the battle at Cul-Dreimhne near Sligo, but only one of Colm's men, who strayed outside the physical bounds of Colm's protection.

As part of the terms of the settlement, Colm was allowed to keep the psalter. The book was given the name Battler and was carried into battle by the O'Donnells, the O'Neill clan that Colm belonged to, as a protective talisman until the 16th century. It is now in the care of the Royal Irish Academy.

Another result of the battle was that Colm was excommunicated, although this was later withdrawn. He was also strongly encouraged to leave Ireland; in effect, exiled. In anger, he vowed that he would never set foot on Irish soil again and went to Scotland, where in A.D. 562 he founded the monastery at Iona, which became the center of Scottish Christianity. In the first recorded mention of the Loch Ness monster, Colm saved one of his followers from the beast by making the Sign of the Cross and ordering it to go away.

In 575, the Convention of Drum Cet was called by High King Aed Ainmire, whose father had fought on Colm's side at Cul-Dreimhne. Three items on the agenda held personal and political interest for Colm: the independence of the Irish colony of Dalriada in Scotland from its Irish rulers; the release of a prisoner who was under Colm's protection; and the proposed expulsion of the poets from Ireland. Colm attended—whether invited or not is uncertain—after conscientiously packing Scottish soil into his shoes so as to remain technically faithful to his vow.

The first two items, significant on that occasion but of little interest now, were resolved to Colm's satisfaction. The matter of the poets, however, is timeless.

The kings claimed, probably with justification, that the power, arrogance, and outrageous demands of the poets had far exceeded their usefulness, and they wanted them abolished. Colm, himself a poet of no small accomplishment, successfully negotiated a compromise in which the poets survived, though with severe restrictions on their privileges. Some later historians feel that Colm's championing of the poets, who were the historians and biographers of that period, is the main reason for his fame.

Colm died and was buried at Iona, but this did not put an end to his travels. A persistent popular tradition says that some time later his bones were taken to Downpatrick in County Down, where he was buried in the same tomb as Patrick and Brigit. It is said that the remains of Patrick and Brigit moved apart to allow Colm to rest between them.

Early in the 9th century, many monks were killed in a Viking raid on Iona, and the survivors fled to Kells, which was expanded to accommodate

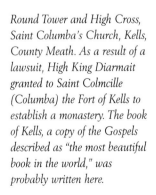

Round Tower and High Cross, Saint Columba's Church, Kells, County Meath. As a result of a lawsuit, High King Diarmait granted to Saint Colmcille (Columba) the Fort of Kells to establish a monastery. The book of Kells, a copy of the Gospels described as "the most beautiful book in the world," was probably written here.

them. Two of the annals report that in A.D. 875 or 877 "the shrine of Colum-Cille, and his relics in general, were brought to Ireland, to avoid the foreigners [Vikings]."

Exactly where in Ireland they were brought to is not stated, but Kells would seem the logical place. However, the *Annals of the Four Masters* report that in 1127 "the shrine of Colum-Cille was carried off into captivity by the foreigners of Ath-cliath [Dublin], and was restored again to its house at the end of a month."

"The shrine of Colum-Cille" was the box containing his relics, but it is also the name of the church, Scrín Cholmcille, on the Hill of Skreen two miles east of the Hill of Tara, a church dedicated to Colmcille and by local tradition his burial place.

It is possible that all these accounts are correct, and Colm's relics rest at Iona and at least two places in Ireland.

> "Like the cure of a physician without light,
> Like the separation of marrow from the bone,
> Like a song to a harp without the ceis [small accompanying harp],
> Are we after being deprived of our noble."
> —*Dallan Forgaill, disciple of Colmcille and Chief Poet of Ireland (d. A.D. 598), on the death of Colmcille.*[8]

The Cursing of Tara

Diarmait mac Cerbaill was the last pagan high king. The annalists deemed it worthy of notice that in A.D. 560 Diarmait was the last to celebrate the Feast of Tara, a pagan ceremony instituted by Ollamh Fodhla in the 13th century B.C., which celebrated the high king's marriage to the earth goddess. Diarmait's reign is seen as the point when Christianity became the dominating influence on Ireland's social structure and morality, and this story dramatically illustrates this important change.

Diarmait's champion went on a circuit of Ireland to make sure the high king's peace was being kept. The method he chose was to enter the fortress of every provincial and local king carrying a spear crosswise in the crook of his arms. If he could not get through the doorway in this manner, it was evidence that the owner had strengthened his defenses in anticipation of an attack. This meant that the peace had been or was about to be broken, and the champion would order the entrance to be widened until it was wider than the length of his spear.

This is what happened when he tried to enter the newly built fort of Aed Guaire, a local king in Connacht. Aed Guaire strongly resented the order to destroy the entrance to his new fort, and so he cut off the head of the high king's champion.

Diarmait ordered the arrest of Aed Guaire. Aed Guaire sought sanctuary (Church protection from civil law) with his brother Bishop Senán. Senán sent him to Abbot Ruadán, and Ruadán smuggled him into Britain. But Diarmait pursued him in Britain, and he returned to Ireland, where Ruadán concealed him in a chamber under his kitchen, spreading straw over the trapdoor.

Diarmait got wind that Ruadán was harboring the fugitive, and he sent a young man to search Ruadán's house. When the youth entered the kitchen, he was struck blind. Diarmait, protected by the divine power of a high king, arrived in person and questioned Ruadán.

"Where is Aed Guaire?"

"I don't know where he is," said Ruadán, standing on the trapdoor, "unless he is hidden under the straw beneath my feet."

Diarmait was deceived and went away, but, having second thoughts, returned and found Aed Guaire. One of his men started to pull Aed Guaire out of the chamber, but his arm suddenly withered, and Diarmait had to do it himself.

This capture was a violation of the age-old principle of sanctuary, which is still in use and can be observed in present-day dramatic stand-offs between government authorities and rebels or protestors who take refuge in a church.

Ruadán organized a hunger strike, another timeless tradition, in protest. Diarmait retaliated with his own hunger strike against the holy men, each side eating only every other day. This went on for a year, until the saints tricked Diarmait by appearing to take food on a day of fasting, whereupon Diarmait broke his fast.

When the trick was revealed, Diarmait became angry at the loss of face and initiated a cursing duel with Ruadán.

> "I pray to God that it is thy church that shall first come to desolation."

Pages 90–91: Hill of Tara, County Meath, looking north. The Hill of Tara was the sacred and political center of Ireland until the sixth century A.D. ©Duchas the Heritage Service.

"May thy dynasty come to naught, and may neither son nor grandson of thine reign in Tara forever!" snapped the saint.

"May thy church lie for ever waste!" said the king.

"May Tara be desolate to all eternity!" said the saint.

"Mayest thou go to thy grave lacking one of thy limbs and an eye!" said the king.

"Mayest thou have an ugly face before thou diest! May thine enemies overcome thee! And may the leg upon which thou refusest to stand up in my presence be smashed to pieces!" said the saint.

"Take Aed Guaire and be gone," said the king: "but may thy church be a center of war continually, even though there may be peace over the rest of Ireland!"[9]

After that, though not immediately, Tara was abandoned as the royal center, although subsequent kings of Ireland retained the title King of Tara. However, Diarmait's son, Aed Sláine, and his grandsons, Diarmait and Bláthmac, became high kings.

Saint Fechin and the Seven Wonders of Fore

Saint Fechin (c. A.D. 585–664) founded a number of churches and monasteries, including the famous Fore of the Seven Wonders, near Castlepollard, County Westmeath. Most people have heard of the Seven Wonders of Fore (*Fobhar*, "spring"), but few can name all of them.

1 "The Monastery in a Bog." So it appears, but the buildings are situated on hard ground in the middle of low, wet land.

2 "The Mill Without a Race." Saint Fechin ordered a watermill built, but the builder argued that there was no running water at the site selected. Fechin told him not to worry, that God would provide the water when it was needed. The builder finished the mill and laughed at Fechin when no water appeared. Fechin crossed the hill to Lough Lene and struck the bottom of the hill. This caused water to run from the lake through the hill to the mill. The builder was caught up in the workings of the mill when the

water started running and was chopped to pieces.

3 "The Water That Runs Uphill." The water that flows through the hill to supply the mill appears to emerge at a point higher than where it enters the hill.

4 "The Tree That Will Not Burn." The tree is an old ash near the abbey. It is also said that only three branches would grow on the tree, in honor of the Blessed Trinity.

5 "Water That Will Not Boil." Water from Fechin's Well is said to be a cure for toothache. But like water from many holy wells, it will not boil no matter how long it is heated. Skeptics who try to boil it anyway will have bad luck.

6 "The Anchorite in a Stone." The anchorite's (hermit's) cell across the valley from the monastery was used until the 17th century. A hermit shut

Saint Fechin's Monastery, Fore, County Westmeath. Established by Saint Fechin as a monastery in the 7th century, Fore was a Benedictine Priory until 1539, when Henry VIII suppressed it. The present building dates mainly from the 15th century.

himself up in it, vowing never to go out the door as long as he lived. One day, he heard hunting horns. A follower of the hunt in his youth, he had an overwhelming desire to watch the action. To be faithful to the letter of his vow, he climbed out a window, but when he was climbing a wall, he fell and broke his neck.

7   "The Stone Raised by Prayer." When the church was being built, the workmen were not able to lift the huge lintel above the doorway, but Fechin prayed, and it miraculously moved into place.

The *Annals of the Four Masters* record these events:

> "A.D. 664. A great mortality prevailed in Ireland this year, which was called the Buidhe Connail ["Yellow Plague of Conall"], and the following number of the saints of Ireland died of it: Saint Feichin, Abbot of Fobhar, on the 14th of February; Saint Ronan son of

Saint Fechin's Monastery, Fore, County Westmeath. Pieces of cloth are placed on this tree near the holy well in petition for favors requested or thanksgiving for favors received.

Bearach; Saint Aileran the Wise; Saint Cronan son of Silne; Saint Manchan, of Liath; Saint Ultan Mac hUi Cunga, Abbot of Cluain Iraird *Clonard*; Colman Cas, Abbot of Cluain Mic Nois; and Cummine, Abbot of Cluain Mic Nois.

"After Diarmaid and Blathmac, the two sons of Aedh Slaine, had been eight years in the sovereignty of Ireland, they died of the same plague."

An uncomplimentary story is told to explain the deaths of so many notable people in that plague.

Ireland was experiencing a population explosion, and the joint high kings, the brothers Diarmait and Bláthmac, appealed to the holy men for a solution. They asked the saints to pray that God would send a plague to kill a great number of common people. Fechin and most of the leading churchmen agreed that this was a good idea, and they set to work.

God evidently heard their prayers, but He answered them in His own way. He sent a great plague, but it spared the common people and killed the high kings and the saints.

The "Saint Ultan" in the mass obituary above is not the Ultán who was related to Saint Brigit and wrote a hymn in her honor (see "Brigit, Saint and Goddess"). Brigit's kinsman was Saint Ultán Mac-Ui-Conchobair, bishop and abbot of the monastery at Ardbraccan near Navan in County Meath, who also died about this time.

Saint Kevin and Glendalough

"I do not know if there is any tune about Glendaloch, but if there be, it must be the most delicate, fantastic, fairy melody that ever was played. Only fancy can describe the charms of that delightful place." —*William Thackeray*, The Irish Sketch-book

"Saint Kevin, you must know, sir, is counted the greatest of all the saints, because he went to school with the prophet Jeremiah."
—*Joe Irwin, 19th century tour guide in Glendalough*

Saint Kevin was 120 years old when he died in the year A.D. 618. He loved animals and was very kind to them, but he didn't like people very much. When he was a young man, he decided to live alone in Glendalough, "Glen of Two Lakes," and think about God.

Kevin lived contentedly in the stump of a hollow tree at the closed end of the glen next to the larger lake, the Upper Lake. He ate the fruits and nuts that grew wild in the glen and dressed in the skins of animals that had died of old age, because he wouldn't kill an animal. The smaller of the two lakes, the Lower Lake, is also called Loch Péist, which means "Lake of the Water Monster." The water monster lived in the Upper Lake at that time, but because Kevin loved animals, he and the monster got on well, and the monster didn't try to eat him.

Kevin used to stand up to his waist in the Upper Lake, which is very deep and cold, and pray with his arms outstretched and the palms of his hands raised to heaven. One day when he was praying like this, a blackbird put a twig into one of his hands, then another and another, until she had built a nest. Kevin loved animals so much that he stood there without moving until the bird had laid her eggs, the eggs had hatched, and the baby birds were old enough to fly away. This is why pictures of Kevin usually show him with a bird in one hand.

No one else lived in the glen at that time, but a local farmer named Dima noticed that one of his cows gave as much milk as fifty other cows. He sent a servant to follow the cow the next morning and find out what she was eating that made her produce so much milk. He discovered that she spent the whole day licking Kevin's feet.

When he reported this, Dima said, "That man must be a saint," and he brought Kevin to his house and cleaned him up and dressed him in regular clothes.

Kevin hated it, but he knew that his discovery was a sign that he was meant to tell people about God. The story about how he was found by the cow gave him a reputation as a holy man, and people came from all over Ireland and from other countries to be near him and listen to him preach.

This was good news for the monster who lived in the Upper Lake, because it meant he didn't have to go far from home to find his dinner. It probably didn't bother Kevin that the monster was eating the people who came to see him, because it made Glendalough less crowded. But the people who hadn't been eaten yet wanted to kill the monster before he could eat them. Because Kevin didn't want him to be killed, he asked the monster to please move over to the smaller lake, Loch Péist, and he gave him something useful to do.

Graveyard with Round Tower, Glendalough Monastic City, County Wicklow. The 34-m (c. 100-foot) renovated round tower (9th–12th century) was used as a place of refuge during attacks. Round towers were always associated with Irish monasteries and served as landmarks for travelers.

Glendalough Lower Lake, County Wicklow. Glendalough (Gleann Da Loch, "Glen of Two Lakes") takes its name from the Upper Lake and Loch Péist ("Lake of the Water Monster"), which is also known as the Lower Lake. Saint Kevin founded a monastery here in the 6th century, which became one of the major universities during the Dark Ages and contributed to Ireland's reputation as "the land of saints and scholars."

The farmers drove their cattle through the Upper Lake to cleanse them of disease. The water from the Upper Lake washed down into Loch Péist, where the monster ate the diseases. They say the monster no longer lives in Loch Péist, and it's probably safe now for people to swim in it, but there is a lake on Camaderry on the north side of Glendalough called Loch na hOnchon. *Onchon* is another word for "monster," and it's possible that the monster of Loch Péist moved to Loch na hOnchon after Kevin died.

Before Kevin's time, Saint Patrick took a tour around Ireland with Oisín son of Fionn mac Cumhaill to hear the stories of how places got their names. When they arrived at Glendalough and Oisín told Patrick about Loch Péist, Patrick asked why Fionn hadn't killed the monster, as he had so many others. Oisín said it was because Fionn knew that Kevin would come along in a few centuries to sort out the problem.

Saint Kevin's Kitchen, Glendalough Monastic City, County Wicklow. Popularly known as Saint Kevin's Kitchen for the resemblance of its belfry to a chimney, this oratory with the steeply pitched stone roof typical of early Irish stone churches is dated to the 11th century or earlier.

*Grave Stones, Glendalough
Monastic City, County Wicklow.*

Kevin lived in the small cave called Kevin's Bed in the face of a cliff 25 feet (8 m) above the Upper Lake. A woman named Cathleen had a crush on Kevin, and she used to annoy him by asking him if she could clean his cave, cook his dinner, warm his bed for him. Kevin avoided women because he planned to become a saint.

One time he stripped off his clothes in front of Cathleen and rolled naked in a bed of stinging nettles, thinking that the sight would disgust and discourage the woman. For some reason it didn't, so he took a bunch of nettles and beat Cathleen with them to drive her away. He probably thought she got the message, but the next day, when he went back to his cave to sleep, he found her there waiting for him. He was so angry that he pushed her out of the cave, and she fell into the lake and drowned.

This tragedy is the reason you never hear birds sing at the Upper Lake. The often quoted first lines of Thomas Moore's version of the story, "By That Lake Whose Gloomy Shore" (1811), refer to this tradition:

> "By that lake, whose gloomy shore
> Skylark never warbles o'er,
> Where the cliff hangs high and steep
> Young Saint Kevin stole to sleep.
> 'Here, at least,' he calmly said,
> 'Woman ne'er shall find my bed.'"

The True Legend of Saint Patrick

The usual story about the national saint is that Patrick drove the snakes out of Ireland, introduced Christianity to Ireland, and was the first bishop in Ireland. None of that is true. There were never any snakes here. Not only does the cool, damp weather keep them out, but when Moses cured Gaedel Glas, the grandson of the inventor of the Irish language, of snakebite, he said, "I command, and God commandeth, that no serpent harm this lad or any of his seed forever; and that no serpent shall ever dwell in the homeland of his progeny."

Serpents are archetypal symbols of the guardians of esoteric knowledge, and the druids were called "serpents." Patrick broke their power, and in that way metaphorically drove the serpents out of Ireland. The druids mostly turned Christian—or claimed to have turned Christian for political expediency—and called themselves poets. Some, like Colmcille, became saints.

Who brought Christianity to Ireland, if not Patrick? Probably refugees from Roman religious suppression on the Continent. There were scattered communities of Christians here when the first bishop, Palladius, arrived in A.D. 431, appointed by the Pope to organize them under his rule. Palladius founded three churches and left after six months because the natives threw stones at him. He didn't speak the Irish language, didn't like to travel, and wasn't very fond of the Irish people either.

Popular belief, supported by the annals, says that Patrick came to Ireland in A.D. 432. According to his autobiography, supported by modern historians, Patrick arrived as the second bishop about A.D. 460. The son of a Roman civil servant living near Glasgow, he was captured at the age of 16 by Irish pirates led by the high king, Niall of the Nine Hostages. He was set to work at Slemish Mountain near Ballymena in County Antrim, looking after pigs. He escaped after ten years and studied Christianity on the Continent for 30 years.

On his appointment as bishop, he landed at Drogheda, on the east coast, and sailed ten miles (16 km) up the River Boyne to the Hill of Slane, a royal cemetery since 2666 B.C. and an important pagan religious site. It was the eve of the First of May, the first day of summer in the Celtic calendar and a major occasion for religious ceremony.

Ten miles away, and in clear sight of the Hill of Slane, is the Hill of Tara, the ancient political and sacred center of Ireland. There the druids of the high king, Leary, were preparing to light the ceremonial first fire of

Hill of Slane, County Meath.
This is where in the year 433,
according to popular belief,
Saint Patrick lit a huge bonfire
that announced the coming of a
new God.

summer. By law, all other fires in the area had to be extinguished and rekindled from the sacred fire at Tara.

Patrick knew about this law, and that is why he lit a huge bonfire on the Hill of Slane before the druids lit theirs. He was brought before Leary to explain.

"I lit the fire to announce the coming of a new God, who is more powerful than your old gods. The new fire of Christianity will never be extinguished."

King Leary was a politician. If what Patrick said was true, he wanted to be on the side of this more powerful god. But he was also a realist.

"If you prove that your new god is more powerful than the old gods, I'll join your religion," he told Patrick.

Of course, this was what Patrick wanted. If the king converted, Ireland would become a Christian country. Patrick proposed a duel.

"Your druids will try to start a fire with their pile of dry wood, and I will start a fire with wet, green wood, by the power of my God."

Leary accepted. His druids were unable to get even a whiff of smoke from their dry wood, while Patrick's wet, green wood spontaneously burst into flame.

Ruins of 16th century church, Hill of Slane, County Meath.

Leary was impressed, but not yet convinced.

"What will it take to convince you?" asked Patrick.

"My great-grandfather's (to the 12th generation) foster father, Cúchulainn, was one of this country's greatest heroes. He died over 400 years ago. If you can bring him back to life, and I'm convinced it is indeed Cúchulainn, I'll join your religion."

"All things are possible with God," said Patrick.

The following morning, Patrick and Leary were standing on the Hill of Tara. They saw a chariot come over the crest of the hill, driven by a warrior in full battle array. The warrior drove up to them and introduced himself as Cúchulainn.

Leary quizzed him about Cúchulainn's boyhood feats and famous warrior deeds and weapons tricks, like throwing a sword up in the air and catching it in the scabbard. The warrior gave all the right answers, and Leary was convinced it was the great hero himself. (Personally, I think Patrick hired an actor. Everyone in Ireland knew the stories about Cúchulainn.)

"Your god is indeed more powerful than the old gods," said Leary. "I'll join your religion."

Patrick planted his crozier (the bishop's staff and symbol of office) firmly in front of him and conducted the baptism ceremony.

When he finished, he said, "Congratulations, King Leary. You're now a Christian."

"Thanks very much," said Leary in a strained voice.

Patrick went to take back his crozier, and he found it was stuck. When he looked to see why, he discovered to his horror that he had driven it through Leary's bare foot and pinned it to the ground.

"Oh, I'm terribly sorry, King Leary," Patrick said, easing the crozier out of the king's foot. "Why didn't you say something?"

"I thought it was part of the ceremony."

Croagh Patrick overlooking Westport, County Mayo. Saint Patrick climbed to the top of Croagh Patrick, Ireland's sacred mountain, and drove the demons out of the country. The ancient religious pilgrimage in commemoration of this event has in the past several years turned into a popular event for young people as a demonstration of their desire for world peace and reconciliation.

Saint Patrick and the Demons

When Saint Patrick climbed to the top of Croagh ("Cone") Patrick in County Mayo for a 40-day fast, he found it infested with demons. He banished them, but one, Caorthanach ("Wild Woman"), the mother of Satan, hid in a hollow and escaped Patrick's curse of expulsion.

She then fled the mountain, but Patrick borrowed a horse and chased her. She poisoned the wells along the way, and Patrick and his horse began to suffer from thirst. The horse fell on the slope of the Ox Mountains at Tullaghan near Coolaney, County Sligo, and Patrick was thrown to the ground. He hit his head on a rock, and water began to flow from the spot.

The imprint of his hand and back and the horse's hoof can still be seen next to the well, which is called the Hawk's Well.

> "He who drinks, they say,
> Of that miraculous water lives for ever."
> —W. B. Yeats, "The Hawk's Well" (1917)

After Patrick and the horse refreshed themselves, they continued chasing Caorthanach north to Lough Derg in County Donegal, where Patrick slew her. Her blood turned the water in the lake red, which is how Lough Derg ("Red Lake") got its name.

Croagh Patrick, frequently called Ireland's sacred mountain, is the scene of a Christianized penitential pilgrimage on the last Sunday of July, which is called Garland Sunday or Crom Dubh Sunday.

Crom Dubh ("Black Hump" or "Black Bent-Over") was the most important pagan god at the time of Patrick's arrival. He is featured in many folk tales as a pagan human lord who engages in verbal and magical combat with Patrick, always losing to the saint, until he is finally baptized.

"Dar Crom" ("by Crom") is an expression still used by Irish speakers. Crom Dubh Sunday has in recent times been partially secularized to a generic peace walk popular among young people.

Lough Derg has been a place of pilgrimage for many centuries. In the Middle Ages, penitents were led into Saint Patrick's Purgatory, a cave resembling a modern amusement park house of horrors, where the devil was literally scared out of them.

Chapter 5

Legends of Kings

The Blarney Stone

"There is a stone there,   A clever spouter
That whoever kisses,   He'll turn out, or
Oh! He never misses   An-out-and-outer,
To grow eloquent;   'To be let alone,'
'Tis he may clamber   Don't hope to hinder him,
To a lady's chamber,   Or to bewilder him,
Or become a member   Sure he's a pilgrim
Of parliament: From the Blarney stone!"

— *"Father Prout" (Rev. Francis Sylvester Mahony), 1834*[10]

"Blarney is baloney sliced thin." —*Anonymous*

Whatever American tourists have heard about Ireland before they arrive, they know that kissing the Blarney Stone at Blarney Castle near Cork City is supposed to confer on them the gift of blarney or gab, although they may not know why, or how the term "blarney" entered the Queen's English.

After they have kissed the Stone, they are usually informed by a mischievous tour guide that the local lads are in the habit of "shedding a tear for Parnell" (the political leader deposed in 1890 because of a sex scandal) over the Stone on their way home from the pub.

Those who have undergone the experience know that it is difficult enough to kiss the Stone because of its position in the parapet of the castle. You have to lie down and kiss the under part. And it would indeed take a great leap of the imagination, let alone a more prodigious effort on the part of the "tear-shedders," to make the tour guide's claim believable.

Here is the true legend of the Blarney Stone and the origin of the term *blarney.*

Blarney Castle, County Cork.

Clíona Ceannfhionn ("Fair-Haired"), a woman of the Tuatha Dé Danaan from Tír Tairngire (the "Land of Promise"), is an Otherworld queen associated with Munster. The O'Keefe family counts her as an ancestress.

Cormac Láidir ("Strong") MacCarthy, who built Blarney Castle in the 15th century, was engaged in a lawsuit. He appealed to Clíona for help, and she told him to kiss the first stone he came upon in the morning on his way to court. He did so—some say it was a stone from a stone circle or a megalithic tomb—and he pleaded his case with such eloquence that he won.

That is why kissing the Blarney Stone is said to impart "the ability to deceive without offending." Concerned that others might gain the same gift of gab from the stone, MacCarthy concealed it by incorporating it into the parapet of his castle.

Unfortunately, according to an investigator writing in 1893, the true Blarney Stone went missing before 1870. In any case, it had only been some 50 years earlier that tour guides had invented the "custom" of the general public kissing the stone. But don't despair if you have gone through the ritual. The 1995 *Brewer's Dictionary of Phrase and Fable* assures us that "a substitute has been provided, which is said to be as effective as the original."

The first Queen Elizabeth is believed to have been the first person to use the term *blarney*, when she so described the "fair words and soft speech" of the owner of Blarney Castle in 1602.

At that time, the Irish Catholic lords were under pressure to renounce their religion and convert to the English Church or have their properties confiscated by the Crown. Blarney Castle was one of the strongest

Kissing the Blarney Stone, Blarney Castle, County Cork. Kissing the Blarney Stone is believed to confer the "ability to deceive without offending."

fortresses in Munster, and so the religion and consequent political stance of its owner were significant.

Cormac MacDermot MacCarthy, the Catholic owner, pretended to be considering "jumping," as the politically expedient nominal conversion to Protestantism was called, and he kept putting off announcing his decision to the Queen with silken excuses. She finally lost patience with his procrastination and exclaimed, "Odds bodikins, more Blarney talk," or, as some have it, "I will hear no more of this Blarney talk. Blarney, Blarney. All is Blarney."

Guaire and Diarmait

Guaire Aidhne was king of Connacht, the western province of Ireland, A.D. 655–666. His royal seat was Durlas, the present-day Dunguaire Castle at Kinvara, County Galway. The poets said his right arm was longer than his left, because it was with the right hand that he gave gifts, and most of the stories about Guaire center on or mention his generosity.

But he wasn't always that way. As a youth, he was so stingy that his people asked Saint Colmcille to do something about his meanness.

Colmcille explained to Guaire that people come into the world without possessions and leave it the same way, and that all wealth comes from God anyway, so it should be shared with all God's creatures. Guaire took the lesson to heart, and with the zeal of the convert became legendary for his urge to give.

Guaire generally amassed the wealth that allowed him to be so generous in ways that were a credit to him. However, cattle-raiding was one of the national sports in those days, and Guaire was an enthusiastic participant.

Groups of young men would nip over the border into the neighbor's territory and make off with herds of cattle and force the owner to pay to get them back. More risky than football, less dangerous than war, it was a way of proving one's daring, sharpening one's battle skills, and pocketing a profit, assuming one survived. Since everyone did it, it was considered more of a nuisance than a serious crime.

But Guaire repeatedly raided cattle from Diarmait son of Aed Sláine, joint high king of Ireland with his brother Bláthmac (A.D. 642–664), and Diarmait declared war in 649. Guaire was soon defeated, and he

was made to submit to Diarmait by kneeling before him and taking the point of Diarmait's sword between his teeth.

Diarmait decided to use the opportunity to test Guaire's famed generosity. He told a beggar to approach Guaire and ask him for a gift.

Guaire, still with the sword between his teeth, gave the beggar his dagger and sheath. Diarmait's men took the gift from the beggar.

The beggar complained to Guaire that the gift had been taken, and could he have another one, please. Guaire took off his jeweled belt and gave it to him. Diarmait's men took the belt from the beggar.

Dunguaire Castle, Kinvara, County Galway. The present Dunguaire Castle was built by the O'Hynes family in 1520 on the site of Durlas, the royal seat of their ancestor, Guaire Aidhne, a 7th century king of Connacht.

The beggar then asked Guaire for another gift. Guaire took off his silver-buckled shoes and gave them to the beggar. Diarmait's men took those.

When the beggar returned to Guaire and told him that the last gift had been taken, a large tear rolled down Guaire's cheek, because he had nothing left to give.

Diarmait took his sword out of Guaire's mouth and said, "Arise, Guaire, and give homage only to Almighty God."

And then Diarmait himself knelt before Guaire.

Guaire and Mochua
The Road of the Dishes

During Lent one year, Saint Mochua, brother of Guaire Aidhne, King of Connacht, was staying next to a well near the small village called Burren in the North Burren of County Clare, five miles from Guaire's castle at Durlas at Kinvara, County Galway.

He was alone except for a young cleric. They were subsisting on one scanty meal a day, which was enough for Mochua. But after some days of this diet, the young man felt a strong craving for meat, and he told Mochua that he was going to Guaire's castle to ask for a square meal.

"That won't be necessary," said Mochua. "My brother Guaire is probably sitting down to his evening meal at this very moment, and he is so generous I'm sure he won't mind sharing some of his food. I'll arrange for a delivery."

Mochua prayed, but apparently he put too much energy behind the prayer. At once the dishes that were just then being set down in front of Guaire leapt from the tables and out of the servants' hands. They flew over the wall and straight along the road to Mochua.

Mystified, Guaire and his retinue jumped on their horses and set off in pursuit of the dishes. When the dishes arrived, Mochua began to praise and glorify God, and he told the young cleric to take his fill of meat. But just then Guaire and his men arrived. They halted their horses and stared in awe at Guaire's dishes on Mochua's table.

The young cleric said, "But look at all the people I have to share it with."

"Not to worry," said Mochua. "I pray to God that my brother and his household will not be able to stir past the place where they have halted until you have had your fill."

With that, the horses' hooves were stuck to the ground, and they were not able to move until the cleric had satisfied his hunger. Then Mochua prayed that Guaire and his people would be released. When they could move again, Guaire came to Mochua and knelt down before him.

"It's all right, brother," said Mochua. "You can eat the food now."

After Guaire had finished the meal, he and his people returned to Durlas. Proof that this story is true is the fact that the five-mile stretch of the road between Durlas and the well where Mochua was staying at that time is still called Bóthar na Miasa, the "Road of the Dishes."

Cormac mac Art

Cormac mac Art, grandson of Conn of the Hundred Battles, was the most famous of the high kings. Although he is often described as a mythical or legendary king, the cautious consensus among modern historians is that he may possibly have been a real person.

Many of the stories about Fionn mac Cumhaill, who flourished through the reigns of seven high kings, are set in Cormac's time. Cormac is credited with much of the landscaping of the Hill of Tara. He also imported the first watermill, which he installed on land east of Tara still called Lismullin, the "Enclosure of the Mill," so that his mistress would not have to grind grain by hand.

Cormac was fishing one time, and he caught a fishhook in his eye. Half-blinded, he was no longer allowed to be king, as a king had to be physically perfect. He retired to a home at Achaill, two miles east of Tara, now called the Hill of Skreen, which is topped by a church steeple that can be seen from Newgrange and the Hill of Slane. Skreen (also Skryne) is the anglicized *scrín*, the Irish word for "shrine," a container for the relics of a saint. The full name in English is the Shrine of Colmcille, because Colmcille's relics were kept there for a time between the 8th and 11th centuries.

Cormac is said to have been the first Christian king in Ireland, a century and a half before the coming of Saint Patrick. One of the annals reports that "he refused to adore the Golden Calf that was then worshipped as God, saying that he would sooner worship the man who made the Golden Calf than the Calf itself, because the goldsmith was worthier than it." For this reason, one of the druids used a magic spell to make a salmon bone stick in Cormac's throat and choke him to death.

Cormac's wisdom is evidenced in what is probably his most famous judgment.

As a child, he was observing the usurper Lugaid mac Con, whom he would eventually replace, during a court session. A widow's sheep had broken into a man's field and eaten the grass. The man demanded that the widow's sheep be given to him in compensation, and Lugaid directed that this be done.

Hill of Skreen, County Meath. Ruins of the 15th century Church of Skreen (Scrin Cholmcille—"Shrine of Colmcille") on the site of a 9th century monastery located on the Hill of Skreen east of the Hill of Tara. Saint Colmcille is said to have founded a church here in the 6th century, and his relics were kept here at one time, hence the name, Shrine.

Cormac, however, objected that this was unjust. Fair compensation would be "one shearing for another," that is, that the man be given one shearing of the sheep in payment for the grass they had eaten.

The people agreed that this was the correct judgment, and Lugaid was forced to concur. This precedent entered case law, was taught in the law schools, and was used to settle local disputes until the 20th century.

The Instructions of Cormac, in the form of a question-and-answer session with his son, Cairbre, are similar to catalogs of advice attributed to Solomon and Odin.

Modern sensibilities may be offended by his long list of detailed warnings about women that includes:

> "Happy is he who does not yield to them!
> They should be dreaded like fire,
> They should be feared like wild beasts.
> Woe to him who humors them!"[11]

But his reply to Cairbre's question "How I shall behave among the wise and the foolish?" is a frequently quoted classic:

> "If you be too wise, one will expect too much of you;
> If you be too foolish, you will be deceived;
> If you be too conceited, you will be thought vexatious;
> If you be too humble, you will be without honor;
> If you be too talkative; you will not be heeded;
> If you be too silent, you will not be regarded;
> If you be too hard, you will be broken;
> If you be too feeble, you will be crushed."[12]

Cormac died in A.D. 277. He had told his followers that when he died he wanted to be given a Christian burial, and that he was not to be interred at Newgrange like the pagan kings.

But Cormac's followers, being pagan, were determined to remain true to custom. They carried his body north towards Newgrange, but when they reached the River Boyne, the river rose against them. Three times they tried to cross, and three times it rose against them, until finally they had to bury Cormac south of the river.

The burial site is called Ros na Ríg, "Hill of the King," and the prominent white house on the hill, which can be seen from Newgrange, is called Rossnaree (Ros na Ríg) House.

Saint Colmcille (A.D. 520–593), the druid-poet who became the third most important Irish saint next to Patrick and Brigit, built a church over Cormac's grave and said thirty Masses for him.

Mound of the Hostages, Hill of Tara, County Meath. This passage tomb, dated 3000 to 2500 B.C., is oriented to the rising sun on November 8 (the First of November by the old calendar) and formed a gateway to the Otherworld on Halloween.

Lia Fáil
The Stone of Destiny

> "The seventh name [of Ireland] was Inis Fáil; and it is the Tuatha Dé Danann gave that name to it."—*from Geoffrey Keating,* History of Ireland

A granite standing stone not native to the area stands on top of the Forrad, a mound where the king's court was located, on the Hill of Tara, the ancient sacred and political center of Ireland. It is known as the Lia Fáil or the Stone of Destiny, and it is one of the four ancient treasures of Ireland because of its ability to verify the legitimacy of the true king by shrieking under him when he stood on it. This was the voice of the Earth Goddess confirming him as her consort, since the king was metaphorically married to the land.

Lia Fáil, Hill of Tara, County Meath. The granite standing stone on the Hill of Tara, the sacred and political center of Ireland until the 6th century A.D., is believed to be the Lia Fáil, the Stone of Destiny, which was brought to Ireland by the Tuatha Dé Danaan.

Conaire Mór, a first century B.C. king of Tara, was certified in this way, but the Lia Fáil fell silent in the following century after Cúchulainn struck it with his sword because it did not cry out under him or his foster son, Lugaid. The next and last time it shrieked was for Conn of the Hundred Battles a hundred years later.

Conn and his druids were walking along the Royal Enclosure, the earthen bank that surrounds the top of the Hill of Tara. He accidentally stepped on the Lia Fáil, which he had never noticed before because it had been toppled and buried, and it screamed so loudly it could be heard for miles around.

The Lia Fáil was unearthed and erected on the Forrad in 1824 to commemorate the rebels who fell in the Battle of Tara during the 1798 Rebellion. An obvious phallic symbol, it probably originally stood at the entrance to the nearby Mound of the Hostages, a Neolithic passage tomb that represents the belly of a pregnant woman.

According to historical records, a 6th century king of Tara, Murtagh, loaned the Lia Fáil to his brother, Fergus, King of Scotland, where it became known as the Stone of Scone. The English stole it from the Scottish in 1296 and put it under the throne at Westminster Abbey, calling it the Coronation Stone. Scottish nationalists stole it back in 1951, but the British government recovered it, finally returning the Stone to Scotland with great pomp and ceremony in 1996.

Modern Irish scholarly opinion insists that the British Coronation Stone is not the Lia Fáil, and no one in Ireland denies that the standing stone seen today at Tara is. The Irish government has never asked the British to return the Lia Fáil, implying that it is not missing. However, descriptions of the Lia Fáil from the 6th century until the 19th century state or imply that it is no longer at Tara.

A key to evidence of a sustained cover-up is to be found at the end of the 13th century *Acallam na Senórach*, a conversation between Saint Patrick and Oisín. In this conversation, Saint Patrick asks Oisín, "Who raised that stone or took it from Ireland?"

Oisín begins, "A high-minded warrior took over the kingdom..."

At this point in the manuscript, the text breaks off abruptly, and we never get Oisín's answer.

This is my theory: When Tara was cursed and abandoned in the 6th century (see "The Cursing of Tara"), the Lia Fáil was buried, if it had not already been buried four centuries earlier.

Murtagh's "loan" of the Lia Fáil to Fergus was arranged as a red herring—probably another stone altogether was loaned—so that some upstart might not use the Lia Fáil to become king and to keep the real stone in Ireland.

This fiction was carefully maintained after the Anglo-Norman invasion in the 12th century to conceal the presence of the Lia Fáil from the invaders. The author of the *Acallam* blurted out the truth, and the revealing passage was torn from his manuscript to preserve the secret. By the time the commemorators of the 1798 rebels dug up the Lia Fáil and planted it on the Forrad in plain sight, even if this made the British aware that they had been tricked, it would have been too embarrassing for them to admit that their Coronation Stone had been a fake all along.

Family Legends

Granuaile and Howth Castle

Grace O'Malley, or Gráinne Ní Mháille in Irish, was born about 1530 and died about 1603. Although her birth and death dates are uncertain, many of the events of her life are well documented in official state papers. This is mainly because she was a major annoyance to the English government at a time when the English were making their final, and more or less successful, effort to pacify Ireland.

Based in County Mayo, she was a shipping magnate, pirate, warrior, and virtual queen of West Connacht. A good portion of her income seems to have been derived from selling "protection" to other shipping merchants. Queen Elizabeth's functionaries variously characterized her as "a most famous feminine sea captain," "a notorious woman in all the coasts of Ireland," and "chief commander and director of thieves and murderers at sea."

She was nicknamed Gráinne Mhaol ("Bald") for the boyish haircut she gave herself when she was denied permission to sail to Spain with her father because she was a girl. It is by the anglicized version of this name, Granuaile, that she is best known today as an almost mythic embodiment of Ireland.

As with many famous and infamous historical personages, legends have accumulated around her name, one of the most enduring of which associates her with Howth Castle near Dublin and still affects the day-to-day operation of the castle.

It is a documented fact that she paid a visit to Queen Elizabeth in London in 1593, presenting herself as an equal in order to complain about restrictions placed on her by Sir Richard Bingham, the English governor of Connacht. Bingham had described Granuaile to Elizabeth as "a notable traitoress and nurse to all rebellions in the Province for 40 years." She obviously impressed the Queen, who wrote to Bingham, "Grany ne Maly hath

Howth Castle, Dublin. The gate of Howth Castle is still left open and an extra place set for dinner because of an agreement with 16th century pirate queen Granuaile.

made humble suit to us for our favour," and countermanded his orders.

The popular version of the Howth legend says that Granuaile called at the castle on her way home from her visit to Queen Elizabeth. But that is not possible, because the St. Lawrence family, owners of the castle from the 12th century to the present day, did not have an heir of the appropriate age in 1593 to fit the story.

This is the true legend of Granuaile and Howth Castle, as related to me by Julian St. Lawrence, the son of the current owner.

In 1576, Granuaile put in to the port of Howth to take on supplies and stopped in at Howth Castle with the reasonable expectation of hospitality from one member of the nobility to another. However, she found the gate closed against her, and the lord refused to receive her, because he was at dinner and did not wish to be disturbed. Furious at the insult, she seized the son of the heir and took him to Mayo.

The boy's father journeyed to Mayo and offered to ransom him. Granuaile refused his money but demanded that the gates of Howth Castle be kept open at meal times and a place set at the table for any stranger who happened to drop in. This strange condition was accepted and the boy was returned to his family.

There is no written verification of this story, thus its classification as a legend. The St. Lawrence family, however, believes it to be true. Since Granuaile apparently put no time limit on her condition, the gate of the castle is still left open and an extra place set for dinner to this day.

A version of this story appears in historical records with a 15th century Burke ancestor of one of Granuaile's husbands in the starring role. An insight into the transmission and interpretation of folklore is provided in the fact that a female biographer of Granuaile feels that the incident actually involved Granuaile and was transferred to the male Burke by sexist male historians,[13] while a male folklorist feels that the male Burke was the protagonist, but the incident was transferred in legend to Granuaile because of her popularity.[14]

Shaun Davey's 1980s recording of the Granuaile suite for uillean pipes and chamber orchestra[15] was immensely popular when it came out and is still frequently heard on Irish radio. During the 18th and 19th centuries, poets used the persona of Granuaile as a symbol of Ireland: "'You need not fret, we'll have freedom yet,' says poor old Granuaile."

But a patriotic song written by Patrick Pearse, the leader of the 1916 Easter Rising, has entered the folk tradition as a true song of the people and

Kildamhnait Castle on a misty day, Achill Island, County Mayo. Kildamhnait Castle was one of Granuaile's strongholds. Achill, connected to the mainland by a bridge, is Ireland's largest island, 13.5 miles long and 12 miles wide (21.6 by 19.2 km). Much of it is either boggy or rocky.

Lynch Wall, Galway City. This is the window from which local legend says Mayor Lynch hanged his son in the 15th century.

has conferred mythic status on the 16th century pirate as an archetypal freedom fighter. The rousing *"Óró, Sé do Bheatha Abhaile"* ("Hooray, Welcome Home") is sung exclusively in Irish, even by non-Irish speakers, and is taught in Irish schools. Sinéad O'Connor includes it on her 2002 album *Sean-Nós Nua*. For Pearse, the song looked forward to a time when Ireland would be independent. For present-day Irish people it celebrates that independence.

The Lynch Wall

I was strolling through the streets of Galway on my first visit to the city in 1978 and stopped to admire an attractive and darkly brooding ancient stone wall on Market Street. The wall backs onto the church of Saint Nicholas, where they say Columbus heard Mass on his way to the New World. Some sort of work was going on. Red numbers had been painted on the stones, and a corrugated metal fence was being erected in front of the wall.

A young woman stopped next to me and said, "Do you know about that wall?" Of course I didn't, so she proceeded to tell me the story.

In 1493, Walter Lynch, the son of the mayor and judge, James Lynch Fitzstephen, was falsely accused of murdering a Spanish man in a dispute over a woman. All the evidence and testimony indicated that Walter was guilty, and the judge had no option but to sentence him to death by hanging.

However, such was the young man's popularity that no one could be found who was willing to perform the execution. As a pillar of the community, Mayor Lynch was keen that "justice" be seen to be done, so he took it upon himself to hang his son from the window of his house—that very window you see in the wall with the skull and crossbones underneath. That incident, the woman informed me, is the origin of the term "lynch" for extra-legal execution by hanging.

As the woman, a native of Galway recently returned from Canada who was refreshing her memories of her hometown, finished telling me the story, the metal fence was completed. I didn't see the wall again for several years. By then it had been dismantled stone by stone and reerected against a strengthening concrete wall a few feet back from the street to protect it from traffic damage. And to allow room for tour groups to gaze in stunned horror while their guides recount the grim tale.

Then I was able to read the inscription:

> "This ancient memorial of the stern and unbending justice of the chief magistrate of this city James Lynch Fitzstephen elected mayor A.D. 1493 who condemned and executed his own guilty son Walter on this spot has been restored to this its ancient site A.D. 1854 with the approval of the town commissioners by their chairman V Rev Peter Daly PP & Vicar of S Nicholas."

I could also see the "1621" on the skull and crossbones under the window, and I read in a local guidebook that the wall and window date from the 17th century, which tends to cast doubt on the veracity of the 15th century story. But by that time, I had learned the "true facts" of the incident: it never happened.

But this made-up legend is one of the most successful examples of tour guide folklore in Ireland, because even the locals are convinced that it's true. By the way, the word *lynch* for unofficial execution derives from the 18th century Captain William Lynch of Virginia, USA.

Máire Rua

Mary MacMahon, known in County Clare folklore as Máire Rua ("Red-headed Mary"), was born about 1615. She was a clever and resourceful, if contentious, member of the local aristocracy. The facts of her life are well documented, but a number of legends have grown around her, none of them complimentary.

Oral tradition remembers Máire Rua as a sinister, lustful brigand and murderer, who married 25 times. Few of her husbands died a natural death. She also kept a male harem disguised as maidservants. A modern tour guide variant says that she took a soldier to bed every night and killed him the following morning.

The real Mary MacMahon was actually married only three times. She and her second husband, Conor O'Brien, completed Leamaneh Castle in the Burren of North Clare near Kilfenora in 1648 as an addition to an existing 15th century tower house.

In 1651, Conor was mortally wounded in a battle with Cromwell's general, Edmund Ludlow, who famously described the Burren as "a country where there is not water enough to drown a man, wood enough to hang one, or earth enough to bury him."

Local tradition says that when Conor was brought back to Leamaneh Castle, Máire Rua said, "We have no room here for dead men." But when she learned that he was still alive, she allowed him to be brought into the castle, where she attended him until he died.

According to legend, she immediately went to General Ludlow or

Cromwell's son-in-law, Henry Ireton, and offered to marry one of his officers, in order to save her lands from confiscation. A man named Cooper was selected, but shortly after the marriage, he had "a nasty accident" with his razor while shaving. She married another officer, who fell from the roof of the castle while inspecting his newly acquired property. The next officer was riding Máire's prize stallion near the edge of the Cliffs of Moher, when Máire whistled a signal to the horse, which reared up and threw that husband over the cliff.

The fact is that Mary MacMahon's third and final husband was a Cromwellian officer named John Cooper, who lived to a ripe old age, though it is probably true that she chose him for the protection offered by his position.

Leamaneh Castle, the Burren, County Clare. Leamaneh Castle, near Kilfenora, is a 17th century mansion built onto a 15th century tower house (visible on the right side of the photo) by the O'Briens and home to Mary MacMahon, the infamous Máire Rua of Clare folklore.

The story about the horse is a variant of the central legend attached to this alleged female Bluebeard.

As a wealthy young widow with extensive properties, Máire Rua attracted many hopeful suitors, and she required them to undergo a test. They had to ride a fierce, untamed stallion to the Cliffs of Moher and return to her castle. None survived the test, because the horse reared and unseated them all, pitching them over the cliff, until a local wise man gave young Turlough O'Loughlin a magic charm. It is also said that his father advised him to use his own saddle and bridle instead of those supplied by Máire Rua.

Turlough mounted the horse, and with the aid of the charm was able to remain in the saddle at the Cliffs. When Máire Rua saw him riding back toward the castle, she closed the gate against him, but he urged the horse forward, and it leapt over the gate. The horse fell and was killed, but O'Loughlin survived the test. The story does not say whether he married Máire Rua, but it is from his feat that the castle is said to have got its name. The Irish of Leamaneh is *Léim an Eich*, which means "the Leap of the Horse." Unfortunately for the credibility of this legend, the district was already named Leamaneh long before this incident is supposed to have taken place.

The historical Mary MacMahon died peacefully in 1686.

The legendary Máire Rua was killed while riding a horse on a stormy night at Toonah Wood, on the road from Ennis to Corofin. Her long red hair became entangled in the branches of a tree, and she was pulled off her horse to be hanged by her own hair. They say her ghost haunts that stretch of the road to this very day.

In a variation of this story, a falling tree killed her as a result of a curse put on her by a widow whose house Máire Rua had ordered destroyed. Yet another ending has her being fastened in a hollow tree and left to starve to death after she had killed the last of her 25 husbands.

Chapter 7

Local Legends and Folktales

The Fairies

Volumes have been written about the fairies of Ireland, some factual, others charmingly imaginative, many nonsensical. The Irish fairies are the Tuatha Dé Danaan, the Irish demigods, reduced in size as they were diminished in importance with the coming of Christianity. Contemporary fairy lore describes them as looking exactly like miniature adults, extremely beautiful, and about the height of a two- to four-year-old child.

The poet William Butler Yeats (1865–1939), who won the Nobel Prize for Literature in 1923, took a great interest in fairy lore and the Tuatha Dé Danaan, especially in his early years.

> "Many of the tales in this book were told me by one Paddy Flynn, a little bright-eyed old man, who lived in a leaky and one-roomed cabin in the village of Ballisodare [County Sligo], which is, he was wont to say, 'the most gentle—whereby he meant "faery"—place in the whole of County Sligo.'"—*from W. B. Yeats,* The Celtic Twilight *(1893, 1902)*

> "'Have you ever seen a fairy or such like?' I asked an old man in County Sligo. 'Amn't I annoyed with them,' was the answer.... 'Ghosts,' said [a skeptic interviewed by Yeats]; 'There are no such things at all, at all, but the gentry [fairies], they stand to reason; for the devil, when he fell out of heaven, took the weak-minded ones with him, and they were put into the waste places. And that's what the gentry are. But they are getting scarce now, because their time's over, ye see, and they're going back.'"—*from W. B. Yeats, Introduction to* Fairy and Folk Tales of the Irish Peasantry *(1888)*

It can be no accident that the site of the great battle of the Irish gods, the Second Battle of Moytura between the old Fomorians and the newly

Coney Island from Rosses Point near Sligo Town. Local people at Rosses Point told Yeats they had seen the fairies dancing.

arrived Tuatha Dé Danaan, coincides with the part of Ireland most associated with the fairies, the area around Sligo Town. Yeats spent a good deal of time in his youth in Sligo, and his early poems celebrate the god-sacred and fairy-inhabited landscape there.

"I will arise and go now, and go to Innisfree..."—*from "The Lake Isle of Innisfree" [Inis Fraoigh means "Heather Island"] (1893)*

"I went out to the hazel wood,
Because a fire was in my head..."—*from "The Song of Wandering Aengus" [of Newgrange] (1899)*

This hazel wood is Hazelwood, a public park on the edge of Sligo Town next to Lough Gill, the lake of the "Lake Isle" of Innisfree.

"The wind has bundled up the clouds high over Knocknarea."—*from "Red Hanrahan's Song about Ireland" (1904)*

The prominent mound on Knocknarea, west of Sligo Town and visible throughout the vicinity, is called Maeve's Tomb, where the queen of Connacht in the *Táin* is believed to be buried. Some stories describe Maeve as the ever-living queen of the Connacht fairies.

"Where the wave of moonlight glosses
The dim gray sands with light,
Far off by furthest Rosses
We foot it all the night,
Weaving olden dances,
Mingling hands, and mingling glances,
Till the moon has taken flight..."
—*from W. B. Yeats, "The Stolen Child" (1889)*

"Rosses" is Rosses Point on the edge of Sligo Town, where local people told Yeats they had seen the fairies dancing.

Most reports of sightings of fairies are just that, with no narrative. Stories as such are rarely set in any particular place. A typical account of an encounter with fairies was written by William Carleton in the stage-Irish language popular in the 19th century. Yeats included it in his *Fairy and Folk Tales of the Irish Peasantry*.

Kitty Corcoran had been an invalid for seven years when a fairy woman suddenly appeared at her bedside to tell her it was her own fault she was sick.

"Arra, how is that?" asked Kitty; "sure I wouldn't be here if I could help it? Do you think it's a comfort or a pleasure to me to be sick and bedridden?"
   "No," said the other, "I do not; but I'll tell you the truth: for the last seven years you have been annoying us. I am one of the good people; an' as I have a regard for you, I'm come to let you know the raison why you've been sick so long as you are. For all the time you've been ill, if you'll take the thrubble to remimber, your childhre threwn out yer dirty water afther dusk an' before sunrise,

at the very time we're passin' yer door, which we pass twice a-day. Now, if you avoid this, if you throw it out in a different place, an' at a different time, the complaint you have will lave you, an' you'll be as well as ever you wor. If you don't follow this advice, why, remain as you are, an' all the art o' man can't cure you."

Kitty, who was glad to be cured on such easy terms, immediately complied with the injunction of the fairy. And the consequence was, that the next day she found herself in as good health as ever she enjoyed during her life.

The Irish Harp

The harp in its modern triangular form is generally agreed to be an Irish invention, there being no firm evidence to the contrary. And, of course, there is a story to go with that claim.

A man was walking along Magilligan Strand in County Derry, and he saw a beautiful young woman sleeping peacefully next to the skeleton of a sea monster washed up on the sand. The wind was soughing melodiously through the ribcage of the monster, and this gave the man an idea. He fashioned driftwood for the framework and braided horsehair for strings in imitation of the ribcage, and when the young woman awoke and saw him there, he calmed her fears with music from the first harp in the world.

The harp has officially been the symbol of Ireland since the 16th century, when it first appeared on coins and the national coat of arms. Modern coins bear a stylized version of the Trinity Harp. The harp has been prominent in Irish myth, legend, and history from earliest times.

The chief of the Tuatha Dé Danaan, the Dagda Mór, played a harp called Uaithne. When the Fomorians stole it from him, he entered their camp by stealth and called the harp to him. It killed nine men as it flew through the air into his arms.

The harper Craftiny is featured in two stories about the 3rd century B.C. king, Labraid Loingsigh.

Craftiny set to music a poem written by the King of Munster's daughter for her lover, Labraid, who had lost the ability to speak. When Labraid heard Craftiny play it, he said, "That is a beautiful song."

After Labraid became king, he was cursed with horse's ears for beating a horse, and a young barber discovered this while cutting Labraid's hair. He risked execution if he revealed the fact, and the strain of concealing such politically sensitive information was making him ill. For relief, he divulged

Mussenden Temple, Magilligan Strand, County Derry. In the 18th century, the Bishop of Derry built a palace on this headland overlooking Magilligan Strand at Downhill. All that remains now is his library, the Mussenden Temple.

Éire by Jerome Connor, Merrion Square, Dublin. One of Dublin's grandest Georgian public parks, Merrion Square faces the National Gallery and Leinster House, where Ireland's legislature, the Dáil, meets. For his depiction of the symbol of Ireland, the sculptor used as a model the surviving neck and forepillar of the 52-string Dalway Harp made in 1621 for the Fitzgerald family.

the secret to a tree. Unfortunately, it was this tree that Craftiny cut down to make a new harp. The tree couldn't keep the secret, either, and when Craftiny played his new instrument for the first time in court, the harp blurted out, "Labraid has horse's ears."

Saint Brigit (c. 439–524) went to visit the King of Munster to ask for the release of a prisoner, but he was not at home. The king's foster father and some of his friends were there, and Brigit noticed some harps. She asked them to play the harps for her. They told her that they were not harpers, and that the harpers were not in the house.

One of Brigit's companions, as a joke, suggested that Brigit bless their hands. She did that, and the men suddenly found that they were able to play as well as skilled musicians. When the king arrived home, heard the music, and learned what had happened, he asked for Brigit's blessing and released the prisoner.

The O'Dalys were poets and harpers from the 13th to the 18th century, and several of the men were named Carrol. One of the most popular and romantic harper stories is about a 17th century Carrol O'Daly from County Wexford. He was in love with Eleanor (Eileen) Kavanagh from County Carlow, but she decided to marry another man. Carrol attended their wedding in disguise and played a love song he had written for her, "Eileen Aroon." She was so impressed that she eloped with Carrol, and they lived happily ever after.

In Bunclody, County Wexford, local people will direct you to a graveyard where she is buried under the name Eleanor Kavanagh. "Eileen Aroon" is one of the songs collected at the end of the 18th century by Edward Bunting from the last of the old-style harpers, Denis Hempson, who died at the age of 112 in 1807. Hempson lived at Magilligan Strand, where the harp was invented.

Continental influences were beginning to change Irish music, and the best known of the new musicians was Turlough O'Carolan (1670–1738), who is considered by many to be the definitive national composer. Carolan was blind, as were many of the great harpers. He composed some 300 pieces, about ten of which are still played by traditional musicians.

There is a story about his most popular composition, "Carolan's Concerto."

An Italian violinist played Vivaldi's new "Fifth Violin Concerto" before an audience that included Carolan. Immediately afterward, Carolan, who, the story goes, could not possibly have heard the piece before, played it perfectly note for note, to the amazement of all. Then he said he could compose a similar concerto off the top of his head, and he played the piece known as "Carolan's Concerto." Then, to Carolan's amazement, the Italian played the piece that Carolan said he had made up on the spur of the moment. In fact, it was a double deception. Carolan had composed it earlier, and the Italian had heard him practicing.

Bunratty Ghosts

The present Bunratty Castle, restored in 1954, was built in 1425 on the site of previous castles. A large blunderbuss is displayed on the wall in the Great Hall. It was fired only once, and then it killed a man. Some say it was the man who fired the weapon. It is said that he is buried in one of the walls, and on the anniversary of his death blood is seen seeping from the wall.

The Main Guard, the room on the ground floor beneath the Great Hall, is used for banquets. One evening a few years ago, three staff members were taking a break in the Great Hall after serving the meal, when one of them noticed a pool of blood forming on the floor. They looked up and saw that the blood was dripping from the ceiling. They cut their break short. During the banquets, the rest of the castle is locked. Nevertheless, footsteps are heard running down the stairs in the locked section every evening.

A maintenance man was using a floor polisher in the Great Hall one night when the castle was otherwise deserted. He told me the plug kept flying out of the electric outlet for no apparent reason every time he turned on the polisher, and he became frightened enough to quit work early.

I was in the Great Hall with a group of young adults a few years ago. Before I had told them any of these stories, or even told them that there were strange stories associated with the castle, one of the girls came up to me with a puzzled look on her face. She had been standing alone in the center of the Hall, when she heard someone breathing heavily next to her. She turned and found no one nearby.

Bunratty Castle, County Clare, at night. Bunratty (Bun Raite) Castle, on the River Shannon, was built in the early 15th century by the McNamara family, but soon became a stronghold of the O'Brien kings (later earls) of Thomond.

An Bacach Rua
"The Redheaded Beggar"

Bridge over the River Nore, Shanahoe, County Laois. This bridge was built with the wealth accumulated by the Bacach Rua ("Redheaded Beggar"), who earned his living begging at the ford replaced by the bridge.

A man and a woman lived next to the ford on the River Nore near the village of Shanahoe, not far from Abbeyleix, in County Laois. One stormy night, they heard someone calling for help, and they went outside to see what the trouble was. A man had found himself stranded in the middle of the flooded river while trying to cross. They rescued him and took him into their house, dried and fed him, and put him to bed.

He was a redheaded sailor who had retired young from the sea with a withered hand and a wooden leg. After he recovered from his ordeal, because he had no family and no home and seemed a decent sort of man, and they had only one son, the couple invited him to live with them. With his withered hand and wooden leg, the man was unable to work, so he spent his days sitting on a stone at the ford and begging from passers-by in order to pay for his room and board. He became a fixture known as *An Bacach Rua*, "The Redheaded Beggar," and the stone where he used to sit is still called *An Chloch* ("Stone") *an Bacach Rua*.

After 40 years, the man of the house died, but the woman told the Bacach Rua he could stay on with her and her son, Terry. Some years later, the life of the Bacach Rua had also run its course, and he lay on his deathbed. The woman and her husband and Terry had often wondered if the Bacach Rua had managed to put away some of his income from his half-century of begging, as they had no idea how much he made apart from what he paid them for his upkeep. So the woman and Terry asked him if he had anything *important* to tell them before he died. He said he hadn't, but there was one last request.

"Bury me with my nightcap on my head," he said.

He died, and he was buried with his nightcap on his head. That night, his ghost appeared, wandering disconsolately through the house and moaning. And the next night and the next night.

"There must be a knot in part of his clothing," the mother said. "The dead can't rest if there is a knot in their clothes."

So Terry got a neighbor to help him, and they dug up the Bacach Rua. Sure enough, when Terry checked the nightcap he discovered a knot in it. He also discovered the reason for the knot: the end of the nightcap was filled with gold coins—30 guineas, amounting to tens of thousands of dollars in today's money. Terry untied the knot but said nothing to the neighbor, and they put the Bacach Rua back in his grave.

"You were right," Terry said to his mother. "There was a knot in his nightcap. I untied it, so the Bacach Rua should rest peacefully now."

He said nothing to her about the gold. That night, he returned to the grave, dug up the Bacach Rua again, took the nightcap with the gold coins, and reburied him.

The following night, the Bacach Rua's ghost again appeared in the house, more agitated than before. Terry told his mother what he had done and showed her the 30 guineas.

"We'll never have peace with that gold in the house," she said. "Take it to the priest. He'll know what to do with it."

Terry took the gold to the priest and told him the story, but the priest didn't want the gold either. He gave it to the County Treasurer and told him the story, and the County used the money to build the handsome seven-arch bridge you can see today across the River Nore just outside Shanahoe, where the Bacach Rua used to sit on the stone and beg.

Clonmacnoise
The Unfinished Round Tower

Clonmacnoise, founded in the sixth century by Saint Ciarán, is one of the most popular monastic sites in Ireland, partly because of the presence of the Cross of the Scriptures, the finest example of medieval high crosses. Of the 75 round towers in the country, built between the 10th and 13th centuries, two can be seen at Clonmacnoise. One is intact and one is not. Whatever the true reason for the state of the unfinished or damaged tower, a local tale that Samuel Lover collected in the early 19th century gives one explanation.

> "You see, sir," said he, "the one down there beyant, at the river side, was built the first, and finished complate entirely, for the roof is an it, you see; but when that was built, the bishop thought that another id look very purty on the hill beyant, and so he bid the masons set to work, and build up another tower there.
>
> "Well, away they went to work, as busy as nailers; troth it was jist like a bee-hive, every man with his hammer in his hand, and sure the tower was completed in due time. Well, when the last stone was laid on the roof, the bishop axes the masons how much he was to pay them, and they ups and towld him their price; but the bishop, they say, was a neygar [tightwad]—God forgi' me for saying the word of so holy a man!—and he said they axed too much, and he wouldn't pay them. With that, my jew'l, the masons said they would take no less; and what would you think, but the bishop had the cunnin' to take away the ladthers that was reared up agin the tower.
>
> "'And now,' says he, 'my gay fellows,' says he, 'the divil a down out o' that you'll come until you larn manners, and take what's offered to yees,' says he; 'and when yees come down in your price you may come down yourselves into the bargain.'
>
> "Well, sure enough, he kep' his word, and wouldn't let man nor mortyel go nigh them to help them; and faiks the masons didn't like the notion of losing their honest airnins, and small blame to them; but sure they wor starvin' all the time, and didn't know what in the wide world to do, when there was a fool chanc'd to pass by, and seen them.

The Unfinished Round Tower at Clonmacnoise Monastery, County Offaly. One of the 75 round towers in the country, this one remains in a partially constructed state. A traditional tale explains why.

Cross of the Scriptures, Clonmacnoise Monastery, County Offaly. This is a replica of the original ninth century high cross, which was moved into the Visitors Centre in 1991. It depicts scenes from the Bible, including the Passion and Death of Christ, the Crucifixion, and Christ in Judgment.

"'Musha! but you look well there,' says the innocent, 'an' how are you?' says he.

"'Not much the better av your axin,' says they.

"'Maybe you're out there,' says he. So he questioned them, and they told him how it was with them, and how the bishop tuk away the ladthers, and they couldn't come down.

"'Tut, you fools!' says he; 'sure isn't it aisier to take down two stones than to put up one?'

"Wasn't that mighty cute of the fool, sir? And wid that, my dear sowl, no sooner said than done. Faiks, the masons began to pull down their work, and whin they went an for some time, the bishop bid them stop, and he'd let them down; but faiks, before he gev in to them they had taken the roof clane off; and that's the raison that one tower has a roof, sir, and the other has none."[16]

Whispering Door, Clonmacnoise Monastery, County Offaly. Carvings of Saint Francis, Saint Patrick, and Saint Dominic are above the 15th century north doorway of the cathedral. A whisper in the doorway can be heard inside the building because of the acoustics.

The Curse of Cromwell

Oliver Cromwell (1599–1658), leader of the Roundheads in the English Civil War, is remembered in Ireland for the brutality with which he solidified the English conquest.

He features in two curses still in circulation among speakers of the Irish language: *"Scrios Chromail ort,"* which means "May the destruction of Cromwell be on you," and *"Mallacht Chromail ort,"* which means "May the curse of Cromwell be on you." The first refers to his nine-month campaign of destruction and massacre in 1649. The second may be related to this short legend.

There had been a prophecy that Cromwell would hold Ireland only as long as he stayed in the country. To help fulfill this prophecy, he ordered that when he died he should be buried in Ireland. When he died, his followers accordingly buried him here, but the Irish soil refused to accept him and vomited his body. They took his body to England and buried it there, but the English soil likewise vomited it. So they threw his body into the Irish Sea, and this is why the Irish Sea is so rough and tempestuous: it is still trying to get rid of Cromwell's body.

Dublin Bay, Sandycove, County Dublin. A view of the Irish Sea from Sandycove. On the far right stands one of the many Martello towers built along Ireland's coast to defend it against expected attacks by Napoleon. Howth Peninsula, north of Dublin, is in the distance.

The Hill of the Hag

The Loughcrew Passage Tomb Cemetery in northwest County Meath comprises the remains of some 30 Neolithic graves (c. 3000 B.C.). They sprawl across a ridge consisting of three hills rising to 911 feet (277 m) called *Sliabh na Cailli* ("Hill of the Hag"). The westernmost and the middle hills are called Carnbane West and Carnbane East. The easternmost is in Patrickstown. In 1836, John O'Donovan, a government surveyor, recorded this local folk tale that explains how the heaps of stones or *carns*—the passage tombs—were deposited there.

A famous old hag of antiquity, called Cailleach Bhéartha (Calliagh Vera), came one time from the North to perform a magical feat in this neighborhood, by which she was to obtain great power, if she succeeded.

She took an apron full of stones, and dropped a carn on Carnbane [West]. From this she jumped to the summit of Slieve Na Cally, a mile distant, and dropped a second carn there. From this hill she made a second jump and dropped a carn on another hill, about a mile distant. If she could make another drop, and dump the fourth carn, it appears that the original feat would be accomplished. But, in giving this jump, she dropped and fell in the townland of Patrickstown, in the parish of Diamor, where she broke her neck. Here she was buried, and her grave was to be seen not many years ago.

This is the very old lady whose shade still haunts the lake and carn of Slieve Gullion in the county of Armagh. Her name was Evlin, and it would appear from some legends about her that she was of De Danannite origin.

She is now a Banshee in some parts of Ireland, and is represented in some elegies as appearing before the deaths of some persons. I know nothing more about her, but that on one occasion she turned the celebrated Fin mac Cooil into a gray old man.

A quatrain of her poetic composition is yet repeated at Carnbane:

"I am poor Cailleach Bera,
Many a wonder I have ever seen—
I have seen Carnbane a lake,
Though it is now a mountain."[17]

O'Donovan described the stone he called "Calliagh Bera's Chair," which is better known as the "Hag's Chair" and "Ollamh Fodhla's Chair": "It is a large stone, about two tons weight, ornamented with a cross sunk (cut) into the seat of the chair, in which three might sit together. This hollow seems to have been made in the stone with a hammer. The cross is probably the work of a modern stonecutter. The back of the chair was broken by some human enemy of old Evlin."

That cross was later identified as a triangulation mark carved by a surveyor shortly before O'Donovan saw it. The "chair" is part of the passage tomb on Carnbane East called Cairn T by archaeologists, widely known as Ollamh Fodhla's Tomb, and locally called the Witch's Cave. Some say the "chair" was used as an altar for illegal outdoor Masses during the penal times in the 17th century. As with many chair-shaped stones at ancient sites, a wish made while sitting on it will come true.

Although the mound is frequently visited by tourists and used for mystical rituals, especially at the autumnal and spring equinoxes when the rising sun shines into the chamber, many local people will not go near the place.

Loughcrew Passage Tomb Cemetery, Oldcastle, County Meath. Cairn T, known as "Ollamh Fodhla's Tomb" and "The Witch's Cave," as seen from the ruins of another passage tomb.

A teenage girl in nearby Crossakeel told me, "The witch will put a curse on you if you go inside the Witch's Cave."

The "lake and carn of Slieve Gullion" mentioned above are the scene of the tale of "How Fionn Got His Gray Hair," and the passage of the tomb there, Cailleach Bhéarra's House, is aligned on Loughcrew. A straight line taken from Slieve Gullion through Loughcrew leads to the Beare Peninsula in County Cork, the Cailleach Bhéarra's home territory, where she was an ancestor goddess. (See "Ollamh Fodhla" for other interpretations of the Loughcrew complex.)

Giant's Causeway, County Antrim.

Killeen Cormac

Killeen Cormac is a round, low-walled mound with trees growing out of it in the middle of a pasture about two miles west of Colbinstown, County Kildare, near the Wicklow border. It is of interest to historians and archaeologists for three reasons: it is said to be the oldest burial ground in Ireland, it contains some of the oldest ogham inscriptions, and it is believed to be the site of one of the three churches founded by Saint Patrick's predecessor, Palladius.

A killeen (*cillín*) is a graveyard for children who died unbaptized. It is also a term used for a pre-Christian burial ground. The Cormac of this story may have been a ninth century king of Munster or the scholar-king-bishop Cormac mac Cuilennáin (d. A.D. 908), whose dictionary of Irish terms is still considered an authority by scholars.

When Cormac died, his followers could not agree where to bury him. So they put his body in an ox cart and let the oxen go wherever impulse directed them. The theory was that the place where the oxen stopped would be the supernaturally appointed site of Cormac's grave. As the oxen were passing Killeen Cormac, a hound leapt from the top of a hill, probably Knockdoo ("Black Hill"), south of the graveyard, and landed on a stone in the graveyard. Cormac's followers took this as a sign that they should bury him there. The imprint of the hound's paw that you can still see on one of the stones in the graveyard is pointed out as proof that this story is true.

In case it isn't true, another explanation of the paw print is that the hound of Glas, in the story of "The Naming of Baltinglass," stepped on that stone during the chase of the demon pig from Tara to Baltinglass.

The Pipers Stones

One of the most accessible and attractive stone circles in Ireland is the one called officially the Athgreany Stone Circle, and locally the Pipers Stones, in a field east of the N81 about two miles south of Hollywood, County Wicklow. Two other "Pipers Stones" lie a few miles to the west of Athgreany.

Several stone circles in Ireland and Britain are called "The Pipers Stones." The story attached to them and to many other stone circles is basically the same. A group of people were dancing on a Sunday to the music of a piper, and God punished them for breaking the Sabbath by turning them into stones.

The Athgreany Stone Circle features an "outlier," a muffin-shaped stone inscribed with a large cross lying a short distance to the east of the circle. This stone was the piper. If you stand at the outlier and look through the circle at sunset at the winter solstice, you will see the sun setting through a gap in the hedge. Several other alignments have been claimed, but this is the most obvious one. Since any circle is a symbol of the sun, it is assumed that all stone circles are in some way related to a sun-centered religion. The name of the Athgreany circle, *Achadh Gréine*, or "Field of the Sun," leaves no doubt in this case.

Catholics see nothing wrong in dancing and playing music and partaking in sports on a Sunday, but many Protestants feel these activities are disrespectful to God and therefore sinful. The Pipers Stones stories associated with Irish stone circles come from the Protestant British tradition, and there is a curious lack of native Irish stories to explain the origin and purpose of these circles.

However, Moyra Caldecott's *Sacred Stones* trilogy[18] published in the 1970s, which is set in Britain during the Bronze Age when the stone circles were erected, illustrates a theory about how the circles work.

Each circle conforms to a constellation, and the local priest, who alone knows the secret, organizes the people to sing and dance around the circle during the night when the relevant constellation is overhead. The movement and sound act like an electrical generator, infusing the earth with energy, which returns in the form of fertility for the crops.

This is the most reasonable theory I have heard about the purpose of stone circles, and it helps to explain the persistence of the widespread folk tale about the dancers being turned to stone. Early Christianity tended to demonize all pre-Christian beliefs and practices. If the people used to dance around the circles before Christianity arrived in these islands, then it must be a form of devil worship. Modern Protestants are more inclined to maintain this attitude than Catholics.

It has been said that if you scratch a good Irish Catholic, you'll find a good Irish pagan just beneath the surface. Many Irish Catholics will agree.

Pronunciation Guide

Pronunciation varies with region and period, for example, the "ch" in "Cúchulainn" is variously pronounced like a "k" or the "ch" in the Scottish "loch" or the "ch" in the German "Ich." The spellings in this book are from all periods, from Early to Modern Irish.

c is always hard like "k"—*ceis* (pron. "kesh")
ch as in Scottish "loch"—Cúchulainn
g is always hard like the "g" in English "gate"—*geis*
s is "sh" before or after "e" or "i"—*geis* (pron. "gesh")
th is "h" except at the end of a word, where it is silent

a = "ah"
e = "e" in "met"
i = "i" in "it"
o = "u" in "but"
u = "u" in "put"

á = "aw"
é = "ay" in "hay"
í = "ee"
ó = "oh"
ú = "oo"

ai = "a" in "that"
ea = "yah" (only a slight "y" sound)
ei = near enough to "e" in "met"
ao = "ee" or "ay" in "hay"
aoi = near enough to "ee"

Pronouncing Irish Names, Places, and Other Words

The pronunciation of the following words is not adequately explained by the rough Pronunciation Guide on page 150. In this section, "kh" stands for the sound of the "ch" in the Scottish word *loch*.

Acallam   AH-gah-lahv

Aed   ay

Aidhne   EYE-nyeh

Almhuin   AL-vin

Aobh   eev

Aoife   EE-feh

Armagh   ar-MAH

Badhbh   bive or bou (as in "bout")

Baiscne   baskin

Bhéarra   VAYR-ah

Bláthmac   BLAW-wahc

Boann   boe-ahn

Bobh   bove

Bóthar   BOE-her

Brighid   breege

Brigid   breege

Caoilte   CWEEL-tyeh

Cathbad   KAH-vah

Cearnach   KYAR-nakh

Cian   KEE-ahn

Ciarán   KEER-awn

Cillín Chaoibhín   killeen khwee-veen

Clíona Ceannfhionn   CLEE-uh-nah KYOUN-in

Cnámros   cnawv-ross

Cuailnge   COOL-nyeh

Cúchulainn   COO-KHUL-an

Cul-Dreimhne   cool DREV-neh

Cumhaill   COO-al

Diarmait   DEER-mat

Dubhtaire   duv-tareh

Emain Macha   OW-en or EHV-en makha

Eochaid   YOE-khee

Eoghan   OH-an

Faughart   FAW-hert

Fedlimid   FAY-lih-mee

Feidhleach   FAY-lokh

fidchell   FIH-khel

file   fill-eh

Fionn   varies: fyoon (rhymes with "good"), fyune (rhymes with "tune"), fyun (rhymes with "fun"), fin

Gabhra   GOU-rah

Goibhniu   GOV-nyuh

Labraid Loingsigh   loury (rhymes with "dowry") lingshee

Laeg   like "like" with a hard "g" instead of "k"

Lebor Gabála   lyour ga-WAWL-ah

Lebor na hUidre   lyour nah hweereh

Luaighne   LOO-eye-nyeh

Lugaid   loo-ee

Lugh   loo

ogham (ogam)   OH-am

ollamh   ULL-ahv

Sidhe Fionnachaidh   shee FINN-ah-khee

sliotar   SHLI-ther

Táin Bó Cuailnge   tawn or toin boe COOL-nyeh

Uillean   ILL-an

Glossary

anchorite A person who has withdrawn into a life of solitude, usually for religious purposes; a hermit.

annals A narrative of events written year by year. Medieval Irish annals blend historical facts and legendary events.

banshee Irish *bean sidh*, "woman of the Sidhe." A woman from the Otherworld who announces and laments the deaths of members of old Gaelic families.

battle goddesses Called the Mórrígna. They are Mórrígan, Badhbh, and Macha. *See* Triple Goddess.

book A miscellany of stories of history, legend, myth, and historical fiction.

brazier A brass-worker.

Bronze Age The period of human history when bronze weapons and implements were used. In Ireland, this was c. 2500 to 600 B.C.

cantred A district comprising one hundred townships.

carn ("cairn") A generic term for a mound of stones. Most Irish cairns cover passage tombs.

Cattle Raid of Cooley See *Táin Bó Cuailnge*.

Colm or **Columba** (the Irish and Latin words for "dove"). A prince-druid who became a saint. See Saint Colmcille.

ceis (kesh), Modern Irish *céis* (kaysh). A small accompanying harp.

Cormac mac Art The most famous of the high kings, renowned for his wisdom. He was possibly a historical figure.

Cormac mac Cuilennáin (d. A.D. 908) Scholar, king, and bishop; he wrote an authoritative dictionary of Irish terms.

Cormac A 9th century king of Munster.

cromlech From the Irish *crom-leac*, literally "a bending or curving of (vertical) flat stones." It is an archaic word for a stone circle or a dolmen. *See* dolmen.

crozier The bishop's staff and symbol of office.

Cruinniuc An Ulster lord, father of the Twins of Macha in the story "The Curse of Macha."

Cúchulainn The archetypal Irish hero and major character of the great epic the *Táin Bó Cuailnge*.

Cucullin A legendary Scottish giant. See "Fionn and the Giant's Causeway."

Cycles of the Kings A collective name for groups of historical legends dated third century B.C. to the 11th century A.D.

Danaan *See* Tuatha Dé Danaan.

Dana Goddess of the Tuatha Dé Danaan.

Diarmait son of Aed Sláine Joint high king of Ireland with his brother Bláthmac A.D. 642–664.

dolmen Breton, "stone table." A Late Neolithic, or more usually Early Bronze Age, tomb comprising three or more flat upright stones capped by a large horizontal stone weighing up to 100 tons. Also called "portal tomb" and (formerly) "crom-lech." As with many ancient sites and artifacts, dolmens are considered the property of the fairies and are generally treated with respect.

druid Irish *draoi*. Pagan poet-priest-wizard.

eric Compensation for a crime. A blood eric is the execution of a murderer demanded by the victim's family.

Fáil See *Lia Fáil*.

fairies Otherworld beings. Irish fairies derive from the Tuatha Dé Danaan, the Irish demigods. Contemporary fairies are described as resembling miniature adults, extremely beautiful, and about the height of a two- to four-year-old child.

Fianna A historical-legendary band of warrior heroes bound by strict codes of honor. Their most famous leader was Fionn mac Cumhaill.

fidchell A board game similar to chess.

file Pre-Christian and Early Christian Irish poet, who combined several social roles: genealogist, storyteller, royal advisor, historian, judge.

filid (plural of *file*).

Fionn Cycle A group of stories centered on Fionn mac Cumhaill, set in the second and third centuries A.D.

Fionn mac Cumhaill (d. A.D. 284) The legendary hero of the common people and focal character of the cycle of stories bearing his name.

Forrad The mound where the king's court was located on the Hill of Tara. See *Tara*.

geis An honor-bound injunction or a taboo.

Guaire Aidhne King of Connacht 655–666, hero of several Irish tales.

hurley Bat used in an Irish game. See *sliotar*.

Inis Fáil "Island of Destiny." The name given to Ireland by the Tuatha Dé Danaan.

Iron Age Period of human history when iron implements and weapons were used. In Ireland, this was c. 600 B.C. to A.D. 500.

killeen Irish *cillín*. A graveyard for children who died unbaptized; also a pre-Christian burial ground.

Knights of the Red Branch Legendary heroic warriors of Ulster, whose deeds are related in the Ulster Cycle set around the time of Christ and centered on the Ulster capital, Emain Macha (now known as Navan Fort), near Armagh City.

Lia Fáil "Stone of Destiny." A granite standing stone on the Hill of Tara brought to Ireland by the Tuatha Dé Danaan, it confirmed the legitimacy of the high king by screaming when he stood on it.

megalith A large, usually rough stone used in prehistoric cultures as a monument or building block.

Mesolithic Belonging to the part of the prehistoric "Stone Age" intermediate between the Paleolithic and the Neolithic periods, beginning around 8300 B.C.

Mórrígan "Great Queen." An aspect of the Triple Goddess: virgin, mother, wise old woman. The Mórrígan is also a member with Badhbh and Macha of the battle goddess trinity called the Mórrígna.

Moytura, the Second Battle of The major set piece of Irish mythology.

Mythological Cycle A collection of Irish stories dated 3000 B.C. to A.D 1.

Neolithic New Stone Age, from 3500 to 2500 B.C. Characterized by the use of ground or polished stone implements and weapons.

ogham also **ogam** The earliest form of writing in Ireland, based on the Latin alphabet, and used mainly between the fourth and eighth centuries A.D. Speculation that ogham was used for magic spells is unsubstantiated.

ollamh Meaning literally "prepared," it was the highest rank among the *filid*. Modern Irish for "professor."

Ollamh Fodhla Poet-king said to have lived in the 13th century B.C.

outlier A stone lying at some distance outside a stone circle.

Paleolithic That part of the Stone Age before c. 8300 B.C., when the Mesolithic begins.

Portal tomb *See* Dolmen.

Saint Brigit (c. A.D. 439–524) Also Bridget, Brigid, Brighid, known as "the Mary of the Gael." Ireland's most famous woman saint, she has assumed attributes of the Irish patron goddess of the arts and the Mother Goddess. *See* triple goddess.

Saint Colmcille (A.D. 520–593) Poet and druid who converted to Christianity. He founded numerous churches in Ireland and Scotland. Also known as Columba.

Saint Fechin (c. A.D. 585–664) Founder of a number of churches and monasteries, including the famous one at Fore in County Westmeath.

Saint Kevin (A.D. 498–618) Founder of the monastery in Glendalough in County Wicklow.

Saint Patrick The patron saint of Ireland, accepted by most historians as having been a real person.

Sétanta Cúchulainn's original name.

sidhe "Fairy mounds." Entrances to the Otherworld of Irish myth.

Sidhe The term used for the Tuatha Dé Danaan after they were banished from the surface of the earth and went to live in earthen fairy or *sidhe* mounds.

skreen (also skryne) Anglicized *scrín*, the Irish word for "shrine." A container for the relics of a saint, often by extension the place where the container is kept. "Skreen" is often part of or short for a place name, e.g., Skreen or the Hill of Skreen near the Hill of Tara in County Meath.

sliotar Ball used with a hurley (bat) in the Irish game of hurling.

Táin Bó Cuailnge: *The Cattle Raid of Cooley* Ireland's epic, describing Cúchulainn's defense of Ulster against invasion by Maeve's army. It is specifically the epic of Ulster.

Tara, Hill of The Hill of Tara was the sacred and political center of Ireland until the sixth century A.D.

triple goddess (1) The female trinity of young virgin, mother, and wise old woman. (2) The trinity Brigit represents of patron of the crafts of healing, poetry, and smithing. (3) The three battle goddesses (called the Mórrígna), Mórrígan, Badhbh, and Macha.

Tuatha Dé Danaan Irish demigods. Stories about them were the basis for fairy lore.

uillean pipes "Elbow pipes." An Irish bagpipe using a bellows held under and worked by the elbow. Producing a sweet, plaintive sound, it is the most characteristic contemporary instrument used for traditional music.

Ulster Cycle Collection of Irish stories dated to around the time of Christ.

Yeats, William Butler (1865–1939) Irish poet, playwright, prose writer. Considered one of the greatest English-language poets of the 20th century, he often used themes of Irish legends in his work. Yeats received the Nobel Prize for Literature in 1923.

Glossary Sources

Oxford English Dictionary, Compact Edition. Oxford University Press: Oxford, 1971.

Boguki, Peter. *The Neolithic Mosaic on the North European Plain*,

http://www.princeton.edu/~bogucki/mosaic.html, accessed May 7, 2003.

www.concentric.com, accessed May 7, 2003.

"Museum of the Iron Age," www.hants.gov.uk, accessed May 7, 2003.

Notes

Many of the early Medieval dates cited in this book follow Dan McCarthy's "Chronological Synchronisation of the Irish Annals" (October 2002):

www.cs.tcd.ie/Dan.McCarthy/chronology/synchronisms/annals-chron.htm

1 From the preface to Dunn, *The Ancient Irish Epic Tale: Táin Bó Cúalnge*, p. xi.

2 O'Curry, *MS. Materials.*

3 Dillon, *The Cycles of the Kings*, p. 118.

4 *Proceedings of the Royal Irish Academy*, 15(1879): pp. 87–88.

5 Condensed from Lady Gregory, *Gods and Fighting Men*, pp. 329–330.

6 "Maeve and Aillil's Pillow Talk" (p. 55) from the *Annals of Clonmacnoise* with original spelling and capitalization: "But the lady Maeve was of Greater Report then the rest because of her great boldness, Buty, and stout manlyness in Giving of battles, insatiable Lust. Her father allowed her for her portion the province of Connaught, and shee being thereof possessed grew soe Insolent and shameless that shee made an oath never to marry with anyone whatsoever that would be stayned with any of these 3 Defects and Imperfections as she accoumpted them, namely with jealousy for any Letchery that she should committ, with unmanliness or Imbecillitie, soe as the party could not be soe bould as to undertake any adventure whatsoever were it never soe Dificult, and Lastly she would neuer marry with anyone that feared any man liveing."

7 My translation from *Triadis Thaumaturgae*, p. 542.

8 *Annals of the Four Masters*, A.D. 592.

9 Macalister, *Tara: A Pagan Sanctuary of Ancient Ireland*, p. 38.

10 Mahony, untitled, as part of the article "A Plea for Pilgrimages" in *Frazer's Magazine*, May 1834. It was appended as the final stanza to "The Groves of Blarney" by Richard Millikin (1767–1815), with "the original Greek" (more blarney).Reprinted from *The Works of Father Prout*, p. 37.

11 Meyer, *Ancient Irish Poetry*, p. 107.

12 Meyer, *Ancient Irish Poetry*, p. 110.

13 Chambers, *Granuaile: The Life and Times of Grace O'Malley*, p. 88.

14 Ó hÓgáin, *Myth, Legend and Romance: An Encyclopaedia of the Irish Folk Tradition*, p. 319.

15 Written by Shaun Davey and performed by Liam O'Flynn and Rita Connolly with song texts in English.

16 Lover, *Myths and Legends of Ireland*, p. 59.

17 *Proceedings of the Royal Irish Academy*, 9(1864–1866): pp. 356–357.

18 Caldecott, *The Tall Stones, The Temple of the Sun, Shadow on the Stones.*

Bibliography and Story Sources

Ball, Francis Elrington. *A History of County Dublin*. Dublin: Royal Society of Antiquaries of Ireland, 1920.

Caldecott, Moyra. *The Tall Stones, the Temple of the Sun, Shadow on the Stones*. London: Rex Collings, 1977; Corgi, 1979.

Chambers, Anne. *Granuaile: The Life and Times of Grace O'Malley*. Dublin: Wolfhound Press, 1979, 1983, 1998.

Colgan, John, *Triadis Thaumaturgae seu Divorum Patricii Columbae et Brigidae Trium Veteris et Maioris Scotiae seu Hiberniae Sanctorum Insulae*. Louvain: Cornelium Coenestenium, 1647.

Davey, Shaun. *Granuaile* (suite), Tara Records 3017.

Dillon, Myles. *The Cycles of the Kings*. Oxford: Oxford University Press, 1946; reprinted Dublin: Four Courts Press, 1994.

Dillon, Myles. *Early Irish Literature*. Chicago: University of Chicago Press, 1948; reprinted Dublin: Four Courts Press, 1994.

Dooley, Ann, and Harry Roe. *Tales of the Elders of Ireland*. Oxford: Oxford University Press, pbk, 1999.

Dunn, Joseph. *The Ancient Irish Epic Tale: Táin Bó Cúalnge*. London: David Nutt, 1914.

"Father Prout." See Mahony, Rev. Francis Sylvester.

Gregory, Lady Augusta. *Gods and Fighting Men*. London: John Murray, 1904; Buckinghamshire, UK: Colin Smythe, 1976.

Hill, Judith. *Irish Public Sculpture: A History*. Dublin: Four Courts Press, 1998.

Jacobs, Joseph. *Celtic Fairy Tales*. Illustrated by John D. Batten. London: D. Nutt, 1892.

Keating, Geoffrey. *History of Ireland* (Forus Feasa ar Éirinn). Early 17th century. Edited and translated by David Comyn and Patrick S. Dinneen. Irish Texts Society, vols. 4, 8, 9, 15. London: David Nutt, 1902–1914.

Lodge, John. *The Peerage of Ireland*. 2nd ed. Revised by Mervyn Archdall. Dublin: Moore, 1789.

Lover, Samuel. *Legends and Stories of Ireland*. London: Baldwin and Cradock, 1832. Reprinted as "Samuel Lover's Legends and Tales of Ireland" in *Myths and Legends of Ireland*. Twickenham, Middlesex: Senate, 1998.

Macalister, R.A.S., ed. and trans. *Lebor Gabála Erenn*, Part Four. Irish Texts Society, vol. 41. Dublin: Educational Company of Ireland, Ltd., 1941.

Macalister, R. A. S. *Tara: A Pagan Sanctuary of Ancient Ireland*. London: Charles Scribner's Sons, 1931.

MacKillop, James. *A Dictionary of Celtic Mythology*. New York: Oxford University Press, 1998; pbk 2000.

MacNeill, Máire. *Máire Rua: Lady of Leamaneh*. Whitegate, County Clare, Ireland: Balinakell Press, 1990.

Mahony, Rev. Francis Sylvester ("Father Prout"). "A Plea for Pilgrimages", *Frazer's Magazine*, May 1834. Reprinted in *The Works of Father Prout*. Charles Kent, Ed. London, Routledge, n.d. [1880].

Meyer, Kuno. *Ancient Irish Poetry*. 2nd ed. London: Constable, 1913.

Murphy, Rev. Denis, ed. *The Annals of Clonmacnoise, from the Creation to 1408 A.D.* Trans. 1627 by Conell Mageoghagan, S.J. Dublin: Royal Society of Antiquaries of Ireland, 1896.

O'Curry, Eugene. *Lectures on the Manuscript Materials of Ancient Irish History. (MS. Materials)* Dublin: James Duffy, 1873.

Ó hÓgáin, Dáithí. *Myth, Legend and Romance: An Encyclopaedia of the Irish Folk Tradition*. New York: Prentice Hall and Ryan, 1991.

Simpson, W. Douglas. *The Historical Saint Columba*. London: Oliver & Boyd, 1963.

Snoddy, Theo. *Dictionary of Irish Artists*. Dublin: Wolfhound Press, 1996.

Thackeray, William Makepeace. *The Irish Sketch-book by Mr. M. A. Titmarsh*, Vol II. London: Chapman and Hall, 1843.

Yeats, William Butler. *Collected Plays*. Dublin: Gill and Macmillan, 1992.

Yeats, William Butler. *Fairy and Folk Tales of the Irish Peasantry*. London: Walter Scott, 1888. Reprinted in *A Treasury of Irish Myth, Legend and Folklore*. New York: Crown Publishers, 1986.

Some of the older sources listed here may be available on the Internet.

Index

Author's Acknowledgments

I thank Dúchas–the Heritage Service, for the use of indicated photos; the staffs of the National Library of Ireland, the library of the Royal Society of Antiquaries of Ireland, and the library of the Department of Irish Folklore at University College Dublin for their help in researching the background to the stories; Nuala Hayes, from whom I heard the little-known story of *An Bacach Rua* ("The Redheaded Beggar"); Julian St. Lawrence of Howth Castle for sharing his family legend about Granuaile; the staff at Bunratty Castle for their true ghost tales; the nameless woman who firmly believed the Lynch Wall legend she told me; Michael Roberts of Moytura, Sligo, for his insights into the great mythological battle that took place in his backyard.

I rely heavily on two touchstones in navigating the intricacies of Irish myth, legend, and folklore: James MacKillop's *Dictionary of Celtic Mythology*, which became an instant classic highly regarded by scholars in the field when it was published by Oxford in 1998, and Dáithí Ó hÓgáin's *Myth, Legend and Romance: An Encyclopaedia of the Irish Folk Tradition* (1991), which is an indispensable compendium of specialist Irish material.

Dr. MacKillop is the editor of the Irish Series at Syracuse University Press and a former president of the American Conference for Irish Studies. Professor Ó hÓgáin, who has published many books on Irish traditions, is a senior lecturer in the Department of Irish Folklore at University College Dublin.

Note: No one mentioned in these Acknowledgments has reviewed this book before publication, and no opinions (except where noted) or errors should be attributed to them.